Alexis de Tocqueville

Alexis de Tocqueville
Threats to Freedom in Democracy

Michael Hereth

Translated by George Bogardus

Duke University Press   Durham 1986

© 1986 Duke University Press
All rights reserved
Printed in the United States of America
on acid-free paper ∞
This book is a translation of Michael Hereth's
*Alexis de Tocqueville: Die Gefährdung der Freiheit
in der Demokratie,* © 1979 Verlag W. Kohlhammer GmBH,
Stuttgart Berlin Köln Mainz, published by agreement with
EULAMA and Kohlhammer.
Library of Congress Cataloging in Publication Data
appear on the last printed page of this book

Contents

Translator's Preface

This book presented an unusual translation challenge in that it was a work in German on French texts for rendition into American English. Fortunately, the author is at home in French as well as German, and has a good grasp of written English. Yet double translation gave unavoidable problems. For instance, he and I decided to use freedom for *Freiheit* instead of liberty, since varying use of both might imply an unintended difference in meaning. Also *Politiker* is rendered as political man rather than politician to describe Tocqueville, to avoid pejorative connotations in modern American usage. Likewise, *praktische Klugheit* appears as prudence, not common sense or practical intelligence. The very rare *Aporie* (*aporia*) became logical impasse, for more immediate impact.

The *liberalism* and *liberal* of the fourth chapter are used in the original and European sense, signifying in their economic aspect free enterprise rather than a tendency toward state intervention.

In the quotations from *Democracy in America*, I used Phillips Bradley's 1980 edition of the earlier Reeves-Bowen translations.[1] The language is often still old-fashioned, but has the virtue of recalling the nineteenth century. For quotations from *The Old Regime and the French Revolution* (*Ancien Régime*, etc.), I mostly used Stuart Gilbert's fine work for its first section, but sometimes translated directly from Tocqueville when my rendering seemed equally good, closer to the original, or more colloquial.[2] The same is true of *Recollections* (*Souvenirs*), translated by George Lawrence.[3] For want of an English translation of *Ancien Régime, Part 2*, I worked directly from the French passages supplied by Hereth. Quotations from Tocqueville's other works, letters, and speeches have perforce undergone double translation.

Preface

In the United States, there is a rich and lasting tradition of attention devoted to the political thinking of Alexis de Tocqueville. In the authoritative *Bibliographie Sélective Commentée* of André Jardin and Françoise Melonio, for instance, well over a third of the described works have come from American pens.[1] This is hardly surprising, since the subject of the French aristocrat's main work, which made him world-famous almost overnight, was the United States of America. And like many Americans of the 1830s, Tocqueville perceived in the American political and social order the paradigm of the new democratic age.

Thus, right from the beginning, his *Democracy in America* aroused great interest in the citizens of the New World. At first, it was the peculiar commentaries of an aristocrat from the Old World which provoked Americans to lively debate over this work; but very soon afterward they began to cite him as a notable witness, and after a while large portions of his book were used as a contribution to formulating the Americans' understanding of themselves in the debate over the American union and Americanism. And the Americans made Tocqueville a citizen of their republic.

In view of this, it is evident that the specifically American debate on Tocqueville's studies and thinking is not primarily concerned with analyzing his gradually changing particular concepts and political symbols, and their meaning—and with putting these into a systematic relationship—as does, for example, the study by the Englishman, Jack Lively.[2] A person who discusses common problems with fellow citizens will naturally clarify these problems, rather than the concepts. Thus it is that since George Wilson Pierson's great treatise, *Tocqueville and Beaumont in America*,[3] practical politics is the main topic of most American studies of Tocqueville. Seymour Drescher's book, *Dilemmas of Democracy, Tocqueville and Modernization*,[4] likewise carries on the tradition of understanding and interpreting Tocqueville as a writer on practical politics, as does the study by Marvin Zetterbaum, *Tocqueville and the Problem of Democracy*,[5] for instance.

Of course, in order to understand Tocqueville as a thinker and interpreter of practical politics and political systems, one must not limit one's self to his book on America. And Drescher's work, *Tocqueville and England*,[6] and Richard Herr's *Tocqueville and the Old Regime*,[7] are noteworthy examples of research in Tocqueville's works from the viewpoint that the French nobleman should be interpreted as a political man.

My book, too, looks upon Tocqueville as a political orator, and in my view his "new political science" is still entirely in the tradition of practical philosophy, which is concerned not so much with attaining philosophical cognition for its own sake, as for the sake of virtuous action and a sound social and political order. For sharply defined explanations of the political symbols employed by Tocqueville, the reader will have to seek in other works for guideposts to interrelations in the history of thought.[8]

American readers probably need no indication of the outstanding introductions to American editions of Tocqueville's works, of which I will name only two out of many: Max Lerner's "Introduction" to *Democracy in America*,[9] which also appeared as a monograph,[10] and the study by Phillips Bradley, which was published as an appendix to the second volume of the book on America.[11]

I was aided in producing this study by all the foregoing works, as well as by the many friends who advised me. Among the many I should like to mention Melvin Richter, who encouraged me, and André Jardin, whose devotion to Alexis de Tocqueville is an indispensable model for me.

The Hamburg State Library and the Beinecke Library at Yale made available to me with laudable generosity the manuscripts at their disposal, and my employer, the Defense Minister of the Federal Republic of Germany, helped decisively in that the Bundeswehr University at Hamburg financed trips to the United States, France, and England, and allowed me a sabbatical that provided me with the leisure to write the final text.

The American translation of this book stems from the intellectual curiosity of my friend, George Bogardus, who proposed to do it. The result fascinates me. My interpretation of Tocqueville appearing in American English remains very familiar, precisely because the writing of the French *homme de lettres* reflects so much of the practical wisdom embedded in English-language idioms.

The result of so much friendly support is a book that attempts to facilitate the reader's access to the works of Alexis de Tocqueville. It is a complement, not an alternative, to the reading of his works. The charm of Tocqueville's writings cannot be duplicated by any interpretative work.

So far as it was possible, I have quoted from the edition of the *Complete Works* being published sporadically under the direction of J. P. Mayer.[12] This edition is now being carried forward by a French commission formerly directed by Raymond Aron. In part, however, I had to resort to the incomplete edition of Gustave de Beaumont.[13]

Introduction

For many readers, critics, or colleagues nowadays, one has to justify writing a book on a thinker of the nineteenth century. For them, there is really just one thinker of the previous century whom one can quote without the necessity of justification, since he is supposed to have solved the riddle of human history. But, they say, he is not Alexis de Tocqueville.

Why then a book about a thinker of yesteryear? Is this not an intellectual exercise in trading antiques, art for art's sake, a game of marbles?

For them, the favorite argument that we can understand our own times better—of course, with conscious effort—if we know their origins in previous times, is incorrect in regard to the particular thinkers analyzed, and unhelpful in regard to Tocqueville, because in this respect a book about Marx or Comte would actually accomplish more. In other words, they have finally succeeded, achieved "social relevance" as it is called, if citation of an author serves as a substitute for direct experience.

But why is the historical line of argument—understanding of one's own time through knowledge about prior times—not correct for our subject author?

First of all, they say, Tocqueville wrote for his fellow citizens, not for our times. Secondly, it would be immodest and conceited to interpret the entire past of mankind as the prehistory of one's own biography, and the entire record of events and processes of human thought as the prehistory of one's own consciousness. With such an attitude toward the past, one is in the strange position of a temporary god. One reaches a temporary peak of historical and mental development, until one dies and becomes humus for the ensuing blossoming of the human mind. Tocqueville is no source of humus.

Yet all these considerations and theses concerning the history of ideas are quite unsatisfactory. They cannot really justify the study of Tocqueville or any other thinker in human history, even though similar justifications can ordinarily be found in introductions to comparable works.

What is it then that makes study of Alexis de Tocqueville seem rewarding to me?

Well, if the history of mankind and its civilizations is probably not a history of finite or infinite progress—which, at least at present and according to one's insight into that kind of progress, has reached its peak in one's consciousness up till now—then very possibly there are ever-recurring problems in human social life, for the understanding and interpretation of which authors in the past also have made sensible expositions.

In the period after the French Revolution, Alexis de Tocqueville experienced the crisis of European societies and held himself aloof from it. And this experience drove him to inquire into the causes of the crisis and to search for valid and stable bases of a new order.

Economic, social, political, and spiritual orders in society are "normally" perceived as self-evident and problem-free. Only when internal or external crises challenge the order do theoreticians of legitimacy, critics, philosophers, or social technicians come forward, and each in his own manner untangles the disorder.

But if disorder is to be perceived as disorder at all, a certain detachment from society is a prerequisite for the person who perceives the disorder, that is, the consciousness of the analyst cannot fully coincide with that of society, or otherwise the disorder would not be perceived. A knowledge of order, which is a prerequisite to perception of disorder and which is present in the mind of the analyst and critic, is expressed in analysis and criticism of concrete phenomena of disorder. Implicitly or explicitly in this criticism, a paradigm of a reasonable order of human social life becomes apparent.

And herein lies for us the exceptional value of the works and writing of Tocqueville. The search for the bases of a reasonable order in a society of equals and the questions regarding the criteria of reasonable community life of free citizens were never stilled in European societies after 1789. Even if we today do not agree with all of Tocqueville's answers, in considering Tocqueville's thought, we are confronted with the problems of order and disorder in postrevolutionary Europe that have given the Western World and its societies no rest till the present. And in these problems we are confronted with a thinker who is fully aware of his peculiar situation. Bound to the *ancien régime* by family and education, he advocated the new opportunities of freedom without losing sight of its dangers.

One is easily disposed to connect much of what Tocqueville expounds with the traditions of the old noble family from which he sprang. And most certainly Tocqueville's concept of freedom is particularly characterized by knowledge of the sovereignty of the old aristocratic class, which freely governed and ruled its serfs. But this is only one side of the coin. Just as noteworthy to me are the ruptures that separate Tocqueville from his aristocratic family tradition. We know that his decision to study the law and to break with the family tradition of *noblesse d'épée* was met with incomprehension.[1] His family's opposition to a marriage with his sweetheart in Metz of bourgeois family surely did not induce loving feelings for the tradition of his family.[2] And after the Revolution of 1830, when the young Tocqueville even took his oath to the new constitution, the scandal in Versailles was complete. In the circles of Legitimists, with which his family was closely connected, he was considered a renegade and was cut off from society.

Tocqueville left this ever more unbearable situation for a

trip to *democratic* America. Afterward he wrote a book on democracy, and finally married a middle-class Englishwoman, Marie Mottley. And even in his political life he refused the support of those who held office and honors in the government under Louis Philippe. After the republican revolution of 1848 he became foreign minister, and when Napoleon III put an end to the republic, he broke off relations with all those who came to terms with the new strong man.

Tocqueville was certainly not esteemed by the French conservatives. And from what he writes about the marriage of a member of the nobility with a member of the bourgeoisie, it can be seen that he is writing not only sociological analysis, but from personal experience. Those who contract such a marriage must break or loosen "the fetters of childish obedience," and they must free themselves from the domination or tyranny of public opinion. "When at length they have succeeded in this arduous task, they stand as strangers among their natural friends and kinsmen. The prejudice they transcended separates them from the others, and places them in a situation that depresses them and embitters their hearts."[3]

Many of Tocqueville's letters, especially at the end of his life, express his loneliness,[4] and his desire for a closer relationship with friends,[5] with whom he maintained extensive correspondence.

The breach that separated Tocqueville especially from the Legitimists, who dreamed of a return of the Bourbons, is apparent also in his comments on the inability of the nobility to accommodate themselves to the developments that had pervaded the *ancien régime*. In parliament he even declared that "the most evil effect of inequality of conditions" and "the spiritual phenomenon, the moral phenomenon, that all aristocracies have displayed is the apparently invincible conviction of a long dominant aristocracy, which insists inequality is just."[6]

It is wide of the mark, in interpreting the works of Tocqueville, to emphasize only the aristocratic tradition of his family. It was precisely from this that he diverged in the course of his life. He knew that he was a citizen bound by family tradition to the past, but was one who accepted the new age of equality and who wanted to participate in it. There was no place for family privilege in a society of equals. Nevertheless, he strove almost unremittingly to remind the old families especially of their responsibility to France. What he guardedly set forth in his introduction to *Democracy in America,* appealing to the upper classes, is expressed much more clearly in his letters to his friend, Louis de Kergorlay: One must make the best out of democracy. In principle, it may not be a good thing. But there is no alternative, and therefore one must take good care of democracy.[7] Louis de Kergorlay, who hoped for restoration of Bourbon rule,[8] seemed to Tocqueville to represent the withdrawal of the old ruling class from society, which he so severely criticized. In his eyes, these old aristocrats were behaving like aliens in society.[9] He warned his friend against a squandered life due to false hopes,[10] and urged him repeatedly not to give in to a melancholy rejection of modern France.[11] Tocqueville urged upon Louis an open mind and activity in society,[12] and in his own plans for a new periodical urged him not to carry on the old debate over the dynastic question, still being continued by the Legitimists. The constitutional situation should be accepted as fact.[13]

In the light of his correspondence with Louis de Kergorlay a whole series of formulations in Tocqueville's published writing takes on an entirely new color. These formulations are the visible portions of the iceberg of the conflict between the nobleman Alexis de Tocqueville and the Legitimists who refused to accept current developments. The attempt to construct a political order on family privilege of the aristocracy or other classes, Tocqueville declared, was doomed to fail from the beginning. The supreme good was freedom. "Therefore all our contemporaries who wish to justify or ensure the independence and dignity of their fellow men must show themselves as friends of Equality. And the only worthy manner in which to show themselves as such is to be one: the success of their sublime enterprise depends upon it." It is not a matter of reconstructing an aristocratic society, but of freedom in a democratic society "in which God has placed us."[14]

In this connection must be seen his warning against a nostalgic, idolizing interpretation of the past. At first, he very skillfully adopts this interpretative attitude, only to reveal its untenability. He himself remembers primarily those outstanding figures of the past who were significant for freedom. He hardly notices the poor and ignorant, the subjects of the aristocracy, and hence he is inclined to judge the past positively. "Yet I comprehend that this fondness was caused by my weakness; since I in my environment cannot see everything at once, I may choose and select from so many things those it pleases me to consider. It is otherwise for the Almighty and Eternal Being, whose eyes necessarily see all things and which clearly see all humanity and each individual simultaneously." Thus, God must look on equality as good, even if, in Tocqueville's eyes, it appears to be a decline. "Equality is perhaps less sublime. It is, however, more just, and its justice constitutes its grandeur and its beauty." And so, in his final chapter of *Democracy in America*, Tocqueville warns against the tendency "to judge the state of society that is now coming into existence by notions derived from a state of society that no longer exists; . . . they cannot be submitted to a just or fair comparison."[15]

This last passage is an unmistakable attempt to persuade the noble ruling class to give up their dreams and to win them over to establishing a democratic republic.

This signifies that, no matter how much Tocqueville's mental universe was influenced by traditions of aristocratic freedom, his endeavors were directed at winning over the French nobility to a new tradition, to a democratic republic. If this attempt should fail, the republic would be abandoned to an individualistic and rapacious upper bourgeoisie, whose indifference to freedom could easily lead the whole society into democratic despotism.

Tocqueville recognized that the stabilization of order in France required great efforts. He sought allies who did not participate in the spiritual disorder, and he hoped to find such allies partly in the old French ruling class, those whose sense of liberty and devotion to the fatherland he could win over to the new republic.

As a young man he lived through the revolution of 1830. He closely followed the establishment and fall of the July Monarchy from 1830 to 1848, as observer and active politician. For a short time the revolution of 1848 made him one of the leading men in the young republic, the threats to which he early discerned and the destruction of which by Louis Napoleon's seizure of power, he was unable to prevent. During the regime of Napoleon III, he remained in retirement from politics until death took him away from a country whose loss of freedom left him a "foreigner" in his own land.

Tocqueville experienced revolution, corruption, unbridled greed, collapse of authority, unstable conditions, tyrannical rule, as well as American democracy, French attempts at establishing stable and libertarian relations, industrialization, and the rise of Socialist ideas in France. Tocqueville perceived and interpreted the crises in his country, not as unique events, but as symptoms of the general crisis of the political and social order of European civilization; and his thinking, like his analyses, typifies the quest for a reasonable order, an order that expresses the freedom and dignity of man. In this search, his inquiring mind attacked core problems of political order in free societies. His unprejudiced questioning, his detachment from current activity, his persistent concentration on the seemingly resolved issue of freedom in democracy made him an archetype of the human quest for a sensible order.

This search forced upon him a detachment from conditions in Europe. He was very reserved toward the current ideologies and proposals for institutional solutions. He knew that only an order that was firmly anchored in the minds of the citizens could bring a halt to the unstable present. Hence, his efforts to define criteria of a reasonable human order were characterized by the attempt to set aside the debris of modern European ideologies—which contributed more to disorder than the establishment of order—and to push forward toward the reconstitution of order in the psyche of the citizens.

Tocqueville's intellectual endeavors are a contribution to the great European-Occidental undertaking, to bring new life to the lost (even for him) sense of order in our civilization.

But for Tocqueville order is no end in itself; the meaning of political and social order is not simply the maintenance of stability and peace. In the second volume of *Democracy in America* he writes: "A nation that asks nothing of its government but the maintenance of order is already a slave at heart, the slave of its own well-being, awaiting only the hand that will bind it."[16] Stability and order make sense only insofar as they are the postulates of men's freedom, which is the true goal of their reflections and political endeavors. The contents of this first chapter are therefore devoted to summarizing Tocqueville's concept of freedom and the knowledge on which the concept is based. Only his concept of freedom makes understandable his thoughts, analyzed thereafter, on constitutions, equality, economy, revolution, and religion.

This first part of the book is concerned with summarizing Tocqueville's search for a reasonable order. His analysis of the United States of America and his criticism of French conditions culminate in the attempt to draw up a paradigm of libertarian order oriented to the American example, a model for the founding of a democratic republic in France. This goal of Tocqueville clearly shows that the author of *Democracy in America* was no ivory-tower professor removed from the world and politics, simply describing curious American and French characteristics.

At the beginning of the second section, we will examine Tocqueville's methodology. This examination will not present various pigeonholes into which one can stuff Tocqueville's works, as has become habitual in modern social sciences, whereby attention to conditions and possibilities of true understanding is largely substituted for true understanding itself. Our subject author is neither a "deductive-empirical" theoretician nor a "normative-ontologist." Most certainly he cannot be fitted over the shoe-trees of "dialectical-historical" theory. In his writings, Tocqueville tried to persuade his readers and compatriots to act in specific ways; he tried to win them over to the democratic republic. The desire to establish a libertarian order in France, or at least to maintain the spirit of liberty among Frenchmen, pervades his studies and presentations. Tocqueville thus belongs to the tradition of political rhetoric, the peculiarity of which is set forth in a digression.

The whole second section of our study is concentrated on Alexis de Tocqueville, the political citizen and an active politician of the July Monarchy and the Second Republic, who pursued in his works perceptibly developing political goals, the struggle for freedom in a democratic republic.

Our presentation is not according to chronology, and makes no claim to describe all of Tocqueville's activities. The simple fact that the documents concerning his activities in local politics are not accessible makes this impossible. The issues we address are more modest: Parliamentary speeches and documents from the daily political struggle are the point of departure for an inquiry that examines Tocqueville in the pursuit of his concept of political freedom under the conditions of day-to-day parliamentary life.

The third part of the inquiry deals with his support for France's conquest of Algeria, one aspect of Tocqueville's conduct that is shamefully ignored in most works treating his thinking.[17]

Not only did Tocqueville not stand aside from the imperialistic ideas of Europe, he contributed to these ideas. In a letter to Henry Reeve of 12 April 1840, he expressed his enthusiasm for Great Britain's imperialist policy toward China as follows: "This is a great event, especially when one considers that it is only the continuation, the last link in a number of similar events in which the European race expands step by step out of its homeland and subjects all other races, one by one, to its empire and influence. In our days something incalculable and extraordinary is going on without our being aware of it, like the establishment of the Roman Empire; the subjugation of four parts of the world by the fifth. Let us therefore not speak so poorly of our century and of ourselves. Men are small, but events are great."[18] It is inescapable that these statements, like his support for France's conquest and settlement policy in North Africa, stand in contradiction to Tocqueville's reflections on self-determination, freedom, and republican government. It is precisely for this reason that they seem to be of special significance.

What Hannah Arendt wrote in another context is true also for Tocqueville: "Such fundamental and flagrant contradictions rarely occur in second-rate writers; in the work of great authors they lead into the very center of their work."[19] And, indeed, the contradictions between Tocqueville's understanding of freedom and his position favoring imperialism indicate for me the limits of his concept of a social order determined by the good of freedom. Thus, our inquiry concludes with a second discussion of his concept of freedom.

As stated earlier, the basis of my interest in Tocqueville is not historical. Rather, it appears to me that the summation of Alexis de Tocqueville's thinking is indeed rewarding, because his new political science raises issues and addresses problems, the serious study of which is meaningful for the analysis and understanding of order in present-day societies. The reading of Tocqueville's writings reveals to the objective student completely new aspects of our modern industrial societies. The issues and problems posed by Tocqueville cannot be put in the usual categories of Right or Left. His inquiries, his criticism, and his concepts of good governance burst the categories of political and scientific schools of thought; even today they still depict new territory lying beyond the staked claims of schools of social science and political parties. Tocqueville's liberalism is, in fact, of a new kind. With rare exceptions, he has not gained followers, either in social science or in politics. His fate has been to be quoted more often than to be read and understood.

I
Freedom in the Republic

THE CRISIS

"Should I assume that the Creator created Man to leave him in an endless struggle with the intellectual wretchedness that surrounds us?" This agonizing question of Tocqueville's in the introduction to *Democracy in America* expresses an almost Old Testament prophetic complaint about the intellectual, moral, and political disorder of his times. Reasonable, virtuous, religious, and peaceful men are the opponents of freedom, while poverty-stricken creatures, fools without virtue or morality, or crass materialists, who talk only of self-interest and not of justice, hold themselves out as the protagonists of modern culture and democratic freedom. "Has such been the fate of the centuries which have preceded our own? and has Man always inhabited a world like the present, where all things are not in their proper relationships, where virtue is without genius, and genius without honor; where the love of order is confused with a taste for oppression and the holy cult of freedom with a contempt for law; where the light thrown by conscience on human actions is dim, and where nothing seems to be any longer forbidden or allowed, honorable or shameful, false or true?"[1]

Tocqueville perceived and outlined the crisis of society of postrevolutionary France of the 1830s. The collapse of the old order in France had made plain intellectual, political, and social chaos that could be seen in the Revolution. In contrast to the United States of America, the Revolution in France missed the chance to found a republican-democratic order. The Revolution did not bring about freedom and a just order; on the contrary, instability, changing regimes, uncertainty, and disorientation were the hallmarks of the state of French society, whose uncertain citizens withdrew more and more from political life. The changes in ruling groups, constitutions, and doctrines determining policy had kept France in suspense since 1789.

When the revolutionaries threw out the Bourbons again in 1830, the country had lived through forty-one years of revolution, regicide, Jacobin Terror, Counter-Terror, the Revolutionary Wars, rule by the people, the attempt at a bourgeois republic, the Napoleonic Empire, wars of conquest, Restoration and its revolutionary overthrow. In these forty-one years constitutions were established, overthrown, and replaced by new ones; new classes rose in the army, administration, learned professions, and the economy, as other classes declined. The army was rebuilt, conquered, was defeated, was rebuilt again. The first evidence of industrialization appeared. Technological innovations began to alter production, the most abstruse social theories and ideologies circulated, found adherents, and were contested in heated debates. The judicial system was radically reformed. France founded colonies. Traditions lost their meaning for conduct; and Gallic Catholicism underwent severe collapse. Everything was in motion. The country was in a state of complete disorientation.

Within a time-span less than that of a human life, horrendous changes had swept across French society. But the citizens had remained. Politically speaking, Paris, France was filled with Bonapartists, Bourbon adherents, Republicans, Jacobins, Socialists, Liberals, Constitutionalists, supporters of a *coup d'état*, Royalists, and a host of ideologists of the most varied kinds. The citizens were faced only with violence and change, which had become synonyms for politics. The seeming peace after 1830 was only the quiet of an exhausted land.

The new rulers of the *juste milieu* had made a gigantic stock corporation of this exhausted France, whose leading class engaged mainly in the pursuit of profit. Selfish interest and advantage were the new hallmarks of the social organization of society.

In his description of the spiritual and political crisis of his country, Tocqueville depicted a society fallen into disorder, which knew not how to make use of the freedom won in the revolutions and civil wars and which was therefore in danger of losing its freedom again in a tyranny. His sensitive awareness of the desolate state of French society moved him to criticize this condition. The seemingly peaceful quiet on the surface could not deceive him from seeing that spiritual and political disorganization was well advanced. France, he saw, like the majority of European countries, was in the midst of a revolutionary process whose outcome could not be determined. It appeared that nothing was valid anymore. Honor, responsibility, law, love of country, and liberty played no role in the new society of the illegitimate heirs of the Revolution.

The Revolution and its varied consequences had radically bared the total lack of a sense of community, of a common good for the citizens of France. France was teetering on the brink of chaos, and the maintenance of outward order could not substitute for the lack of sense of community in the citizens. The maintenance of external order did not extinguish the intellectual and political crisis; it only served to bury the actual disorder, which could erupt at any time.

Tocqueville's efforts were directed toward a new postrevolutionary order in the French republic, and he was thoroughly convinced that this new order could not be erected through institutions alone. Institutions had secondary importance. "There is nothing absolute in the theoretical value of institutions, and their effectiveness depends almost always upon the original conditions of the social state of the nation which applies them."[2] In this connection, it is important that Tocqueville uses the word "social" to signify what the citizens "share in common,"[3] that is, he was looking for a common basis for order and not common private interests. He knew these interests were insufficient in the long run, for in certain situations they divided people. Tocqueville was speaking of an order that is fixed in the thinking, the conduct, and the habits of citizens. Tocqueville saw freedom as being a common good beyond these interests, and leading man beyond them. It "can lead our minds away from small thoughts,"[4] and as a good shared by all can guide the thinking, the actions, and the behavior of the citizens.

Could disorder and crisis in society be subdued by the good of freedom through the orientation of the citizens, its institutions, and all society?

This peculiarly moving, exacting requirement forces the question as to what Alexis de Tocqueville understood by "freedom" that plays such an important role as the common good in ordering society.

FREEDOM

When we speak of freedom nowadays, citizens, politicians, and theoreticians think primarily of freedom *from* something. Some speak of freedom from poverty; others are thinking of liberation from political or intellectual guardianship; and still others think of private spheres of action in which no one has a right to intervene, when they speak of freedom—the freedom of the entrepreneur to manage the means of production and the freedom of the consumer to buy the things he wants.

For Tocqueville, all this is obviously at most a prerequisite for freedom, but not freedom itself.

When Tocqueville writes of freedom, it is more than an institutional sphere for acting as one desires, it is more than an external or private concern. Albert Salomon rightly points out this broader content of what Tocqueville means by the symbol "freedom," and speaks in his analysis of "existential freedom," which characterizes the thinking and conduct of the great Frenchman.[5] And indeed, if Tocqueville prizes freedom, demands it, fights for it, defends it, he intends more than a sum of legal guarantees or constitutional articles that guarantee protection of the individual from harm, or that set forth the authority of the legislature, the executive, the courts, parties or other institutions, and the limits of their power to act and decide. All these freedoms are certainly conditions for the citizen's free life in society, but not identical with freedom itself.

For Tocqueville, living in freedom is a special way of life, which, guaranteed by the constitution and legal system, guides the communal life of citizens and includes the basic attitude of the citizens and their representatives.

The loss of freedom as a deficiency

For Tocqueville, this existential quality of freedom becomes crystal clear in the last phase of his life, when Napoleon III established his tyranny. Tocqueville's descriptions and comments on the state of France that had lost freedom illuminate how sorely he missed freedom. Tocqueville answered Napoleon's brutal destruction of the republic not only with his complete withdrawal from any political activity, but also with his letters and memoranda setting forth how he and his nation had been robbed of a sphere of life that is for him a basic quality.

Oppression, restriction, sadness, discouragement, disgust, and mistrust are the words he employed to depict his feelings over the loss of freedom. He made clear how much he personally suffered from this loss. Not only abstract principles had been breached, the practical way of life of the free citizen had become impossible.[6]

Those contemporaries who allowed themselves to be compensated by the dictator for the loss of freedom by opportunities for economic advantage and professional careers were the objects of his greatest contempt. With few exceptions, he broke off relations completely with those acquaintances who came to terms with the dictatorship of Napoleon III.

For him, France and the French had been corrupted by the usurper, and he felt alienated from his fatherland. He felt, as he wrote to his friend Gustave de Beaumont on 1 October 1854 after his return from Germany, how little territory has to do with "fatherland." Traveling to the [French] border he was overcome with sorrow, and he had to resist the desire to turn back. France without liberty was for him an oppressive experience. What disturbed him particularly was how content the French were in their servitude and how ready they were to subject themselves.[7] He reported to his friend the superficiality of social life and the lack of any seriousness, so that no one felt seriously about anything. "One of the saddest consequences of this regime is it has made this nation both greedy and frivolous. Whoever is not engaged in making money dishonorably, proceeds furiously to throw it away in the maddest ways."[8] The loss of free political life of the republic had robbed France of basic substance and made it a frivolous society, devoid of reality, in which lack of freedom was compensated by surrender to the passions of greed and foolish dissipation.

The free way of life

One cannot be persuaded that it would be possible to acquire the concept of freedom, if one does not know it through practice,[9] wrote Tocqueville in the second part of *The Old Regime*, and thus indicated that for him the word freedom signified a most particular way of life, which presumes legal guarantees, but goes far beyond these.

For him freedom was a practical matter, which could be described in theoretical discourse only with the greatest difficulty. Since, moreover, Tocqueville was obviously aware of the fact that in various societal and historical situations this way of life of practiced freedom may take on the most varied forms, he never attempted to define freedom in general concepts. On the contrary, he wrote that others should not press him to analyze the taste for freedom: "one must feel it himself . . . ,"[10] precisely in practicing it. Although Tocqueville refused to delve more deeply into the sentiment of freedom in analytical concepts, he always bore in mind the fact that the citizen's political freedom of which he spoke comprises various components that cannot be separated from one another without making imperceptible the conjoint and practical character of freedom.

For one thing, it is a matter of the subconscious disposition of the free person, whose attitude and way of life are determined by the "love of freedom," and the "taste for freedom," (*goût de liberté*), and the "pleasure in being free." A free man knows that he is not dependent upon other persons but (only) on God and the Law[11] and manages himself the affairs that affect his own destiny.[12]

The free man who is filled with this love of freedom considers it a good so precious and essential that no other could make up for its loss, the enjoyment of which comforts him in any misfortune (*de tout*),[13] and this prevents him from subordinating it to the pursuit of wealth or other external goals.

It is unmistakable that behind this concept of a free way of life stands the image of the free aristocrat, who lives his life dependent on no one. This also explains why Tocqueville continually reverts to the aristocracy in discussing political freedom.[14]

But Tocqueville was well acquainted with political activity and political freedom not only indirectly through the aristocratic tradition; as a member of parliament, partaker in communal politics, and cabinet minister, he devoted a large part of his life to political activity, and thereby experienced the charm of freedom. His manner of writing on freedom was also an exposition of the personal experience of an active politician. Freedom was for him the actual practice of political activity in the republic. And when he wrote in a letter to Henry Reeve, that the love of freedom and human dignity were his only passions,[15] he expressed not only a central thought of his works, but equally his personal purpose in life in the free activity of the republic. As Marcel writes, "he loved activity, and he wanted to leave his trace on this earth."[16]

With the example of La Rochefoucauld, Wolf Lepenies has showed in what a seemingly insoluble situation the French nobility found itself before the Revolution, superseded in its political functions through centralization and bureaucratization.[17] Oriented toward activity by training and tradition, the French nobles, stripped of their power, were damned to inactivity by absolutism. Salons, literature, and court etiquette were only a shallow substitute for the lost local, regional, and "national" political functions of the nobility, leaving a feeling of melancholy and "worldlessness" in this segment of society, acutely conscious of tradition and politics.

Tocqueville's efforts to seize the opportunity for an active life as a political citizen, presented anew by the democratic republic, appear to me to stem from his deep awareness of the unreality of a nobility condemned to inactivity.[18] To one such as him, who accepted democracy's demands of equality, the Revolution afforded the opportunity for political activity that had been lost long before 1789.

But for him it was not a matter of restoration of the rule of the nobility. That had disappeared long before the French Revolution, and Tocqueville did not mourn it. If he uses the example of the nobility in explaining his understanding of liberty, he refers not to rule of the nobility over the people, but to the collaboration of the nobleman with those like himself in conjoint activity in an aristocratic republic in which aristocrats would be political citizens of the republic independent from each other and from the king.

In other words, the activity bound up with freedom is what interested Tocqueville.

The noble despoiled of his privileges would in this manner take on an important function. He could be a model of the free way of life, who by his example would encourage free citizens to emulate him, who through his actions would invite others to similar conduct. "A class which has taken the lead for centuries has acquired through this long and uncontested usage of its eminence a certain pride of heart, a natural self-confidence in its strength, the habit of being respected, which makes it the point in the social body most capable of resistance. It not only has manly virtues itself; it also reinforces by its example the manly virtues in other classes."[19]

Tocqueville welcomed the opportunities for free activity brought by the Revolution and kept his distance from salons and scholarly life. From 1836 on he worked hard for an active political career. After his first unsuccessful attempt, he was elected to parliament in 1839 and plunged eagerly into political activity.

His main goal was political activity, not intellectual or literary fame. He considered himself a political man and citizen, and his intellectual activities were almost always the result of his enforced inactivity. His detachment from the Bourgeois Monarchy produced his trip to the United States, and his rebellion against unjust treatment of his friend Gustave de Beaumont, which caused him to resign from his professional career (he resigned as a protest against the action taken by the minister of justice to withhold an appointment), gave him the free time during which he produced his work on democracy in America. When the possibility of political activity appeared, he stopped his intellectual researches in large measure.[20]

Once in parliament, he renounced plans for a great new publication supporting his public offices, and only when he was again prevented by external circumstances from playing an active political role did his *Souvenirs* (*Recollections*) and *L'Ancien Régime et la Révolution* (*The Old Regime and the French Revolution*) appear. It is important to emphasize Tocqueville's way of life directed toward politics, for this, it seems to me, is the key to his idea of freedom, which is a freedom for politics and activity. And precisely for this reason, it is so difficult to arrive at a deep understanding of it through theoretical analysis.

The constitution of freedom

When Tocqueville speaks about the freedom and independence of men, "who are free or worthy to be so," he speaks of the "manly and noble pleasure of being able to speak, act, and breathe without restriction,"[21] and so makes it clear that this freedom is not something which exists outside society.

Not the individual separated from society is free, but the person in society. For in any case, speaking and acting have a meaning only among fellow citizens. Freedom leads men to act together and "unites them each day through the necessity to hear each other out, to persuade each other, and to be pleasant to each other in conducting common affairs."[22]

This, however, is not possible by itself. In order that the custom of men's free cooperation can become fixed, citizens must combine in a very distinct manner, as equals. This signifies that freedom of citizens oriented toward speech and activity requires very distinct institutions that make possible cooperation of the free and equal. The republic, for that is what he meant, requires a public area of activity accessible to every citizen.

The aristocrats had practiced liberty among themselves and *vis-à-vis the* king. They ruled their subjects, and the latter did not know freedom and were entrusted to the care of their masters. This is not the place to discuss whether Tocqueville's ideas concerning the benevolent care of the nobility for their subjects conform to reality. What is significant for our discussion is rather the fact that Tocqueville, while fully recognizing the rights of all citizens to freedom as just,[23] directed his attention to the fact that citizens in a democracy can replace the care of the nobles with that of their own organizations. This is the fundamental idea of the democratic republic.

Whereas in earlier times the aristocrat, as the "natural" representative, took "benevolent and quiet interest . . . in the welfare of the people," "the voluntary association of the citizens . . . might then replace the individual authority of the noble"[24] and assure to all the right to a free and common configuration of living conditions. Society would be organized in innumerable free public areas of civic cooperation. The citizens would work together, for "alongside the right to act by themselves, the most natural privilege of Man is that of joining his efforts with those of his fellow men and acting together."[25]

pose not
again as fears
NA
of corps
Freedom in the Republic 21

In his presentation of free areas in French society before
the Revolution, Tocqueville adduced the communities, the
guilds, and *corporations* (professional associations) in which
the citizens themselves freely decided matters. This presentation is precisely the same as that of a public arena. "Here each
appeared upon a stage, small indeed but brightly lit, and always had the same audience ready to applaud or to whistle."[26]
In other words, in the guilds, the *corporations*, and sometimes
in the communities of prerevolutionary France there was a
public arena in which the citizens openly deliberated their
common affairs.[27] This common arena of public deliberation,
which Tocqueville rediscovered in the associations, parties, and
communities of America, is where freedom is practiced. Here
the citizen can come forward to discuss common affairs with
his equals, *die res publicae*, and acting jointly with his fellow
citizens, take his own fate in his hands. He can be free in society.

But the social order, and this has to be re-emphasized, fixes
only the external conditions, the public arena that brings the
citizens together and assures legal procedure, order, and civil
rights. The content of freedom lies in self-government, the
cooperation of equals, and the love of freedom itself, which is
a love for acting in a self-reliant manner to determine one's
own fate.

Also the aims the cooperating citizens pursue are not im-
material. If they are driven by the desire to enrich themselves,
or to strive for riches and profit, they can easily lose sight of
the sense of community of citizens in society. The way of life
reduced to pursuit of prosperity is one possible outcome of
freedom, but should not be confused with it.[28] Only when
citizens wish to maintain their free institutions, for the sake of
freedom and political activity itself, do their basic attitude
and practical activity correspond with order in the republic,
whose purpose for Tocqueville lies in freedom of political
activity. In other words, freedom, as Tocqueville understands
it, in contrast to the liberalism of our times, is not freedom

from politics, is not the presence of a number of reserved areas of private or economic activity. Freedom is freedom for political citizens to act and perform.

Our analysis, which started from Tocqueville's practical experiences in the crisis and his search for order, has shown so far that freedom must shape the legal and constitutional order as the determining good of an ordered society since it guarantees the citizens' free rights. In addition, the social order must be oriented to the highest good, in order to keep freedom tangible, to make possible the citizen's public discussion and acting together with fellow citizens, and the citizens' consciousness must be oriented to the highest good, freedom; they must be motivated by the love of freedom. The practice of freedom is only possible when all three conditions are present together. Then only is the whole greater than the sum of its parts: a freely ordered and self-governing society constituted for the common cause, the free discussion and actions of the citizens managing affairs themselves.

THE INSTABILITY OF A FREE SOCIETY

It will be recognized at once that such a society is a highly volatile political entity. The author of *Democracy in America* knew that the citizens' love of freedom could have two sources: "enlightened self-interest which acknowledges that in freedom one can pursue all possible goals, and the love of freedom for its own sake." The appeal to enlightened self-interest, which can be helpful in accustoming citizens to the practice of freedom, is an important instrument of politics. But the citizens' realization that one can pursue his own separate goals in a free society is not sufficient security for freedom. The danger can easily arise that the citizens believe their particular goals can be reached without freedom, or even that freedom may, for example, hinder their pursuit of wealth.

This last conclusion is decisive for Tocqueville in later life, author of *The Old Regime and the French Revolution*, who had lived through the collapse of the Republic of 1848. He bitterly asserts that private interests are never enduring or obvious enough to maintain love of freedom in the hearts of men, if the taste for freedom for its own sake is not present. Whoever loves freedom for the advantages it brings lacks something for safeguarding freedom. "What is it? The very feeling of being free."[29]

One should never forget, declares Tocqueville, that the taste for freedom is present in all men, but "it has first place only in the hearts of a very few."[30] These, and only these, guard their freedom so jealously, because they love it for its own sake, and not for other advantages.

This brings to the fore one of the central problems of an unideological analysis of modern democracies. How can that love of freedom, "the common source not only of political freedom, but of all manly and high virtues,"[31] be supported and remain effective in a nonaristocratic society, if traditions and the example of the nobility disappear? The majority of men do love freedom, but this love is central, decisive, for only a few. If in a democracy the desires, opinions, and goals of the great majority prevail, there is a danger that freedom will be sacrificed by that same majority for other goals.

Thus, in a democracy it is essential to ensure that the other desires, opinions, and goals of the majority do not come into contradiction with freedom, and *also* that the pursuit of them in freedom will be seen as advantageous, so that those, too, who prize other goods above freedom will not want to renounce it.

Stated otherwise, only a small number of citizens love freedom for itself. The great majority of citizens love freedom, but only in addition to other goods that are at least as important for them. There is always the danger that this majority will feel that freedom hinders or is harmful to the pursuit of other goals, and will sacrifice it for the sake of the other goods. Freedom is endangered, because it is not the supreme good for all citizens.

For this reason, the social and political constitution assumes special significance for the maintenance of freedom. The constitution must be so designed that existing morals, customs, and habits, as well as political institutions, teach citizens the usage of freedom; that the advantages of freedom will be apparent to the citizens, and their extant, although weak, love of freedom will be promoted and strengthened.

LOCAL POLITICS, POWER, AND FREEDOM

But how should a political society be constituted to make freedom possible for its citizens? Which particular institutions are desirable or necessary? How should power be apportioned, how must jurisdictions be defined, and how must the structures and organization of this society be designed?

We have already demonstrated that the idea of freedom, as developed by Tocqueville, has an eminently practical dimension. Freedom presents the possibility of determining in action one's own destiny and of beginning a new one. The emphasis lies on action and is completed by the obvious fact that the destiny of one person is closely connected with the destiny of the society in which he lives. A person so self-sufficient that he needs nothing from society is either an animal or a god.[32]

Neither the image of an isolated individual nor the concept of a fully integrated member of the group in a "collective" actually interprets the reality of persons in society correctly. On the one hand, every citizen in a society needs the society for the achievement of his civic possibilities, but on the other hand, the manifold ties of a person in society do not describe the total reality of the person who by serious thought transcends society, by acting begins something new, and brings it into the world. It follows that human and political freedom consists neither in liberation of the individual from society with its habits, pressures, and institutions, nor in insight into any kind of inevitabilities or "laws" of future social development. People are truly neither gods nor especially clever animals, and it is certainly not their purpose in life to become such. They can be free in society but not out of it. A conscious detachment from concrete events in social reality and criticism of certain circumstances misleads intellectual and thinkers particularly into misunderstanding, to regarding detachment and criticism as freedom itself. According to this viewpoint, freedom becomes intellectual withdrawal from society, and in the end it remains inconsequential and nonbinding, or induces intellectual fantasies. In actual fact, detachment and criticism are simply preconditions for free activity that will be made whole in concrete situations in society.

These insights lie behind Tocqueville's reflections, whose thinking cannot be interpreted by the cliché alternatives of "individualism" or "collectivism." This means that freedom, especially political freedom—and Tocqueville, too, sees it so— is closely connected with the conjoint action of citizens in society. It comprises the conjoint management of public affairs, and it requires a public arena accessible for the citizen.

Aside from the first problem that only a minority of persons love freedom for its own sake, there is a second caused more by the sheer size of the national state than by the citizens' goals and desires. This is that the political unity of the modern, large-sized state seems to be inappropriate for making access to public life possible for more than a small minority of citizens. The more markedly a political society concentrates powers of decision and authority in a central government, the smaller is the number of citizens who have real access to public life.

In fact, the constitutional development of the new, modern nation-states has brought it about that the form of political freedom oriented to practical activity, envisioned in Tocqueville's reflections, is not present in the daily environment of the citizens.

Modernization and centralization

In the sixteenth and seventeenth centuries constitutional development in continental Europe led to extensive monopolization of politics and power in the central governments of the nation-states, in large part owing to the influence of the religious civil wars. In France, especially, the nobility was shorn of power in favor of the dynasty, robbed of its functions in local government, its authority, and autonomy, and bound to the court.[33]

The doctrines of sovereignty of the political science of a Bodin or Hobbes accompanied and fostered this development just as did the rise of national economies and the growth of central bureaucracies. The model of a rational art of government and administration to be admired at that time was not the English political system with its "inefficient," "irrational," and "medieval" structures and procedures, but France.

To do exactly as the French court did, or at least to imitate it, was the desire not only of mistresses of provincial princes, enamored of fancy attire and craving pleasure palaces; government functionaries, political thinkers, and enlightened intellectuals oriented their thinking and desires toward the French model. France was, so to say, the modern and progressive model of enlightened governmental art, which one aped if one wanted to be "up to date." One did. The "modernization" of government and political order in France, which entailed the shift of power from the Estates and guilds, brought about the removal of municipal privileges and rights of self-government, and led to the draining or destruction of regional self-government, was for large parts of Europe the model to imitate.

Then, when the idea of democratic self-government by citizens burst forth as a consequence of the American and French Revolutions, and also when the nearness, duration, and uproar of events in France supplanted in public awareness the case of America with its different outcome,[34] revolutionaries and theoreticians were faced with a landscape of internal politics which forced them to address the new ideas of democracy at the national level of representation of the whole society. In modernization à la française as in the administrative state of Louis XIV and his successors, it became apparent that something had been lost, the *pouvoirs intermédiaires*, the lack of which became painfully apparent after the Revolution of

1789. Local and regional rights of self-government of the nobility, the guilds, the cities, churches, universities, and *corporations,* etc., had been drained away or abolished. The remainder fell victim to the revolutionaries. The slogan *"La nation uni et indivisible"* was directed not only against parties, cliques, and classes, but also against the remains of decentralized government itself. The abolition of power of the nobility and guilds washed away the remains of the structures that under the central government had placed authority to decide near to those who were thereby affected. The decentralized institutions were not democratized, but abolished.

The revolutionaries of 1789 were fully aware of the lack of *pouvoirs intermédiaires* and the prior loss of experience in politics and opportunity to act. The Constitution of 1791 in which the citizens of France tried to assure to themselves the freedom won in the Revolution was characterized by a radical decentralization of power and by the shift of authority to local and regional areas—and we know how short was its life. The central authority, legacy of the Bourbons, triumphed before the latter returned to France. The sovereignty of the monarch was replaced by the sovereignty of the people. It remained sovereignty *over* the citizens, even though established by them.

"Democratization" exhausted itself in creating a political order in which holding office in the central authority was determined by the general voting of the people. Rule of the people became "elective despotism," as Jefferson in America called it, recognizing the danger—the selection of the ruler by the people, not structured self-government by the people.

But why should a citizen of a country consider freedom of action worth striving for, why should conferring and acting with his equals in the political sphere be worth cherishing for a citizen, if he does not know this form of practical freedom?

Posing the question makes clear that with either centralization or decentralization we are addressing a problem that has a close connection with Tocqueville's idea of practical freedom. So it is not surprising that the idea of decentralized order and criticism of centralization plays such an outstanding role in his works, his letters, and his speeches. He knew that decentralized constitutions of society "multiply to an infinite extent opportunities of acting in concert for all the members of the community,"[35] that they thus give the citizens the possibility of experience in active political freedom.

Decentralized order

Long before his trip to the United States, Tocqueville formulated the outlines of his ideas of freedom and the capacity to act in society, in a letter to his friend Gustave de Beaumont, dated 5 October 1828—ideas that run like a red thread through his whole thinking. "In the organization of a nation one must avoid two disadvantages; either the whole power of society is united at one point, or it is distributed in its parts." If there is too much concentration of power at the center, the entire society is put in danger. "When power is distributed, the capability of acting is obviously hindered, but resistance is everywhere." One could say, he told his friend, that a centralized nation will accomplish greater deeds, but will exist only for a shorter time.[36]

As a result of his experiences in America, Tocqueville modified considerably what he termed earlier in 1828 the ability to resist distributed throughout society. Decentralized trial by jury, local self-government of communities, counties, federal states, free associations of citizens, that is, local autonomy within the Union, were recognized by Tocqueville as free spheres of activity for the citizens and as the essential prerequisites for a democratic republic, which make free self-government by the citizens its central concern.

Tocqueville knew that the decentralized system of government of the old feudal order had been destroyed long before the Revolution. The dissolution of the small spheres of local decision, aimed at the enfeeblement of the nobility, the political class of the *ancien régime*, threatened to bring about the most dangerous imbalance in society. All the authority and jurisdictions of the local rulers had been drawn to the central government, which (and this was true also before the Revolution) became the heir of all the authority to decide heretofore distributed throughout the country. In the Enlightened Monarchy, the central government became the entity responsible for and deciding everything. Tocqueville condemned the government of Louis xvi as follows: "For long the Government had suffered from an evil, which is like an incurable and natural malady of forces, which had undertaken to command all, to foresee all, and do all. It had become responsible for all."[37] For one thing, this responsibility for everything led to an excess of demands on the central government, the recipient of the most varied complaints and pleas and contradictory demands, which consequently became the common enemy of society in the eyes of the people, because it could not satisfy their often conflicting expectations.[38] Likewise, this hostility against the royal government, like the exaggerated expectations placed in it, was evidence of general absence of responsibility, which people must grope for in a society whose members do not decide their own affairs.

The development of modern techniques of government with their centralized administrative bureaucracies in enlightened absolutism led to enfeeblement of classes, local entities, and *corporations* with the consequence that all powers of deciding were taken over by the ever intact central government. This was not a peculiarity to France; the same was true for broad regions of continental Europe. "I, like you, note the progress of centralization in Germany," wrote Tocqueville to Beaumont in 1854. "How could it be otherwise? The governments alone are prepared to inherit the old feudal rights, now dying out, certainly not the people. It is not surprising that the sphere of activity of individuals and *corporations* is steadily reduced, while the sphere of the central administration is extended. The growing equality of conditions continues inexorably when once established in a country whose citizens never had or no longer have the habit of jointly taking their affairs in hand and the difficult skill of doing it successfully."[39]

The governments alone were prepared to take over the old feudal rights, certainly not the people. Tocqueville perceived the difficult dilemma that must lead, particularly in France, to the depoliticization of society despite all democratic revolutions. Despite high praise by democrats, the centralized structure of government inherited by the revolutionaries was not suited for the real transfer of power and responsibility to the people, if all local privileges and rights of self-government were taken by it, and not transferred by the nobility to the citizens.

The local world of direct experience

It is obvious that this critique of centralistic concentration of power or depiction of the advantages of distribution of power is not concerned with a pure principle of government. The question of constitutional distribution of authority, responsibilities, and powers between central, regional, and local institutions in society concerns not only juristic constitutional structure. What is at issue is rather the environment felt by the citizen. Why should a person develop a sense of civic responsibility for public affairs, when experience tells him that public and common concerns of his city or region are decided by civil servants, who answer to the central authority and not to him? How should dwellers in a community learn the political virtues of justice, prudence, adherence to reality, love of freedom, and regard for the common cause, if the practice of these virtues is impossible?

Certainly, citizens in a republic are not empty husks into which any constitutional proponent can stuff any political content he wants. Yet it is obvious that the citizens' opinions, attitudes, insights, and customs are not immutable quantities. Traditions can be upheld or neglected. Virtues can develop only in a context that permits or promotes their practice. Citizens are educated in republican virtues and responsibility, responsibility toward fellow-citizens and in free self-reliant management, through actual, first-hand experience, not only through textbooks, teaching, and schools. Citizens in a society will, above all, feel that this is their society and that a republic is their political system, when they learn to practice freedom of action in a republic as their freedom. The principle of distributed and decentralized power stems from persons in society, who are not, as the Physiocrats taught, intellectuals. Not love of humanity, but interest in the solution of current problems can motivate the citizen to responsible action, and the practice of responsible action in the local area makes persons consciously responsible, free citizens of the republic.

The problem addressed by Tocqueville has remained until the present day one of the central problems of organization in societies with democratic constitutions. Citizens actively participating in the political life of a republic require other forms of political organization than those the democrats inherited from absolutism, if democracy is truly to be more than occasions to applaud competing ruling groups.

If the citizens guarantee and ensure for themselves (as against the central government) only voting rights and rights of influence through the constitution of their democratic society, their votes, desires, interests, and opinions must indeed be respected by the central authorities. But this situation does not create opportunities for free and responsible action by the citizens. This means that the citizens' way of life in a democracy and its application to politics cannot change for lack of practice. The practical experience determined by superiors—now elected—does not allow the formation of a specific sense of responsibility for specific problems, since it clears no area for the practice of consciously responsible action.

The majority of people in society, not primarily interested in upholding and developing their freedom and the order supporting it, are solely guided by private and economic interests. In specific situations, they tend only in small degree to precision in their decisions, whether in legal questions, in constitutional questions, or civil rights. The danger is then always great that civil rights of minorities will be disregarded, that principles of the rule of law will be too hastily removed, that occurring problems will be seemingly smoothly settled by disregard of existing rules of procedure and constitutional procedure, or by hasty changes, if large masses of people, with their aroused passions, actively intervene in political life.[40]

There are two ways to prevent the invasion of irrationality into politics:

First, the democratic equality of citizens is restricted to the private sector, while a political elite with the help of a multifarious administration takes care of the problems of politics and the social order, and is only concerned with regular approbation. This alternative only seems to solve the problem. The assumption, in itself irrational, that the central administration semi-automatically guarantees reason, has no proof whatsoever and is disproved by much experience. Moreover, this creates a "bourgeois" society deprived of political practice, which impinges its private interests on political institutions.

Or, secondly, the citizens are educated to the task of shaping their own destiny, shaping policy themselves, by use of their own reason, and control and discipline of their passions. But this educational task is decidedly not primarily the task of a society's schools and educational systems, however important may be their contributions in this respect. Rational, well thought out, and responsible action is less (and certainly not exclusively) the result of teaching than the result of experience and habit. The ethical virtues of pondered, responsible, intelligent and just actions are the result of habituation.[41]

This signifies that in the second alternative the quality of democratic order is decided by the extent to which existing habits can be made useful for a democratic order, the extent to which daily, self-evident practice educates citizens for their task, and the extent to which political institutions accustom citizens to rational use of their rights and possibilities. "Virtues grow in us neither from nor against nature. We are trained by nature to grasp them, but then are made complete only by fixed habit."[42]

Both alternatives for the constitution of a democratic society run through all of the works of Alexis de Tocqueville.

The first alternative, monopolization of politics by a political administrative elite that takes care of a disinterested and privatized society of citizens through central institutions, and regulates and governs it, deprives citizens not only of freedom, but leaves them no sphere in which they are responsible for their actions, and consequently is no republic of free citizens. Such a constitutional order allows democracy to flow into despotism that knows no freedom for the citizens. Tocqueville's experiences in France afford the material for his analysis of democratic despotism.

The second alternative, a decentralized political order, distributes power in society, accustoms citizens to the use of their liberties, and so educates them to the republican virtue of responsibility and participation in the life of the community. Tocqueville saw this alternative as having been accomplished in the paradigm of the United States of America. According to Tocqueville, the Americans had succeeded in warding off the dangers to freedom in a democracy by a republican constitution.

THE PARADIGM OF THE UNITED STATES
OF AMERICA

So far, we have been engaged in analyzing and clarifying the thinking of Alexis de Tocqueville aimed at a libertarian constitution in connection with the European experience familiar to him. The central first culminating point of his theoretical endeavors, the trip through the United States of America, has remained largely untouched.

Today there is a large body of material at hand that shows that both his reflections on constitutional politics and his concept of political freedom already existed at least in rudimentary form when Tocqueville left with his friend, Gustave de Beaumont, for America in April 1831 to study America for a year.[43] But it must not be overlooked that the half-thought-through and surmised thoughts of the great theoretician of modern democracy were clarified and brought to their final formulation by his studies, experiences, and information gained in the United States of America. These were the experiences that enabled him to compose his great work *Democracy in America*. Ralf Dahrendorf is quite correct when he writes "that Tocqueville had France in mind when he traveled through America," even though it would be incorrect to speak of a "program for the future France."[44] Also, Manfred Henningsen's insistence is right "that he . . . sought to fit America into a common European denominator,"[45] but, like Dahrendorf's comment, does not do justice to the paradigmatic purpose in his theoretical endeavors.

Tocqueville wrote about America but meant France. This does not mean that he wanted to transfer the American constitutional system to France. Rather, he became acutely conscious through his American experiences of the miserable state of his fatherland, theretofore only indistinctly sensed. Tocqueville makes this clear many times.[46] The detachment from France provided by the trip to the New World, and the experiences in America permitted him to recognize on his return the reality and practical problems of order in France with a detached, yet participating attitude. Now Alexis de Tocqueville, who all his life had opposed speculative designs of contrived models, had experiences in America at his disposal which put him in a position to declare to the Legitimist enemies of democracy, his private social environment, that it could work in another way.

The trip to America was more than an aid to detached observation. Tocqueville, who came from a country shattered by crises, came to know a political order that, unlike France, had combined democracy and political freedom. Hence, in Tocqueville's reflections French experiences and insights on America were juxtaposed in a paradigm of rational democratic order that allows us to select those elements in his thinking in the book on America which are characterized by his aim to educate the French to democracy.

Tocqueville's book on democracy in the United States is not an analytically descriptive work, designed to describe curiosities on the far side of the Atlantic or to make understandable the workings of American democracy to curious Europeans. The reader of the treatise can indeed satisfy his curiosity, but right in the first volume of *Democracy in America* the reader is confronted with European, that is, Tocqueville's own, and above all, French experience.

Like his second great work on the *ancien régime*, his first is in its whole arrangement not only analytical or comparative; it has a peculiar quality of going beyond this, which sets it apart from most of the contemporary publications of political scientists. His researches on the United States of America and comparisons with France are not only depictions of the workings and settled principles of American democracy, they are also a contribution to formulating principles of modern democracy. They are the original interpretation of an exponent of a democratic, libertarian republic in the struggle to establish a republican order in Europe, who makes use of a description of America to hold up the symbols and principles of a democratic republic, to clarify and develop them himself, and so promote the cause of the republic.

I am convinced that this peculiarity of being not only a description, but part of, the self-interpretation of a democratic regime, aside from its highly informative and analytical qualities, accounts for the great fascination Tocqueville's work engenders still today.

But what is this order for the establishment of which Tocqueville strives to win the reader?

Local politics as education toward freedom

"A nation may establish a free government, but without municipal institutions, it cannot have the spirit of freedom."[47] It is with these words that Tocqueville justifies beginning his analysis of the United States with an analysis of communities. The power of free people rests precisely in the communities; they make freedom accessible to the nation, and awaken in it the taste for freedom as the nation becomes accustomed to it. The reason why local politics and extensive distribution of power among the citizens are indices of the predominance of the spirit of freedom lies in the settled customs and manner of thinking that are fostered by a decentralized system.

His criticism of centralized European nation-states makes clear that Tocqueville perceives a connection between the political constitution on the one hand, and the manner of thinking and the customs of the citizens on the other. "I believe," he writes, "that a centralized administration serves only to enervate the nations in which it exists, for it constantly diminishes their local spirit. A centralized administration can, to be sure, assemble all available forces of a people at a given time and place, but it harms the renewal of forces. . . ."[48]

Tocqueville's conclusions are not based on "modern" categories like "administrative efficiency" or "uniformity of living conditions," which mostly characterize present-day debate, but on the experiences of the citizen, which determine his political consciousness. The possibility of citizens' participation and political activity must be upheld.

If we now clearly observe "that the affections of men generally turn toward power" (*où il y a de la force*),[49] we can, of course, conclude that the offices of the federal government of the United States of America bestow on the officeholders power and fame. "[B]ut these individuals can never be very numerous," and access to these offices is very small. "Such cannot be the permanent aim of the ambitious."[50] To the extent, however, that decisions are made outside the central government, other paths are open in political activity and public esteem—in local politics. "The New Englander is attached to his township, not so much because he was born in it, but because it is a free and strong community of which he is a member, and which deserves the care spent in managing it."[51]

In the township the citizens work together in a local semi-autonomous republic and manage their affairs, instead of executing or modifying the orders of the central administration. "The township of New England possesses two advantages which strongly excite the interest of mankind: namely, independence and authority. Its sphere is limited, indeed; but within that sphere its action is unrestrained."[52]

This freedom of movement makes the township an attractive political sphere. "The native of New England is attached to his township because it is independent and free: his cooperation in its affairs ensures his attachment to its interests; the well-being it affords him secures his affection; and its welfare is the aim of his ambition and of his future exertions. He takes a part in every occurrence in the place; he practices the art of government in the small sphere within his reach; he accustoms himself to those forms without which liberty can only advance by revolutions; he imbibes their spirit; he acquires a taste for order, comprehends the balance of powers, and collects clear practical notions of the nature of his duties and the extent of his rights."[53]

The citizen is not taught his rights, liberties, and opportunities by communication and "theoretical" instruction, but learns them in the course of exercising them. Political action and active participation in public affairs thus become a part of the way of life and customs of the citizen. Liberty becomes practical.

Participation in local politics, which provides practical experience to all citizens and not only to chief administrators and leading politicians, becomes in this way a constituent part of the process of self-education in political society, which continually renews the citizens' spiritual and political strength through their own experience. Self-government in the township, the right and practice of the citizens to join together in associations to solve common problems,[54] free parties,[55] and public opinion[56] make the citizens active, responsible members of society. Through the right of trial by jury they become trained in the application of their laws, which they feel are their laws, which are entrusted to them, and for the application of which they are responsible.[57]

Multiple free institutions and daily practice of political activity make the American republic the concern of the citizens. "The free institutions enjoyed by the inhabitants of the United States and the political rights of which they so regularly make use, constantly remind every citizen in innumerable ways that he lives in society. They turn his mind continuously to those thoughts that it is the duty as well as the interest of men to make themselves useful to their fellowmen; and because he has no special reason to hate them, being neither their slave nor ruler, his heart is easily inclined to benevolence. At first, he becomes concerned with the public weal out of necessity, then later voluntarily; what was calculated becomes instinctive, and by steadily working for the good of his fellow citizens, he at length acquires the habit and taste to serve them."[58]

The actual situation in America serves Tocqueville as a model of a republican political system that through practice makes citizens its supporters. Habit, inclination, and experience promote the love of freedom through practice; collaboration on common affairs, to which the individual was perhaps induced at first only by calculation of advantage and utilitarian considerations, assumes through the events experienced by the citizens themselves in their activities a quality of its own, which is worth striving for in itself. Not utilitarian considerations, but political activity itself becomes the basis of collaboration. Politics and common political activity bind the citizens to the community. Americans help each other, answer for each other, and create a community because they have become accustomed to do so through their practice of politics. The founders of the United States of America thereby accomplished the "task of bringing fellow citizens together . . . and teaching them to manage their own affairs in common," which, not accomplished in prerevolutionary France, presented an obstacle for reasonable political conditions.[59]

With these thoughts, Alexis de Tocqueville burst the narrow bounds of utilitarian interpretation of political order and political activity, already prevalent in his time, which perceives nothing more in politics than the pursuit of private and economic goals extended into society. Political activity is depicted as a sphere of human activity in its own right.

In this connection Hannah Arendt points out that the Americans obviously knew "that public freedom consisted in having a share in public business and that the activities connected with this business by no means constituted a burden, but gave those who discharged them in public a feeling of happiness they could acquire nowhere else."[60] Tocqueville recognized this taste for freedom (*goût de liberté*), which takes its goal as the joy of public activity, as the decisive prerequisite of the American Republic, which draws its citizens into political life, and so makes it possible for them to experience freedom and makes tangible the charm of freedom.

The distribution of power

The portrayal and interpretation of a decentralized political system, developed by Tocqueville in the paradigm of the American union and local political life, indicate several peculiarities that do not correspond with prevailing concepts in the social sciences of today. Tocqueville's works make explicit a different conception of administration and self-government and of citizens' participation in politics. It is based on an entirely different concept of political power, which makes understandable the foregoing concept of political freedom in the republic.

Decentralized politics

In order to make clear that his criticism of the centralization of the European nation-states is not founded on an illusionary concept that everyone is competent for everything, Alexis de Tocqueville distinguishes between two kinds of public affairs: (1) affairs which are the common affair of all parts of the nation "like the enactment of its general laws and the maintenance of its foreign affairs"; [and] (2) affairs which are of interest for only particular parts of the nation "such, for example, as the affairs of the several townships."[61]

Centralization of affairs of the first kind, which Tocqueville calls "centralization of government," he believes to be desirable. He cannot, he says, imagine "that a nation could live and flourish without a strong centralization of government."

But he looks entirely differently upon the concentration in a central government of authority for decisions concerning local affairs, termed by him "centralized administration"—which phrase has given rise to misunderstandings up to the present day—a concentration "which is fit only to enervate the nations in which it exists," because it incessantly diminishes their local spirit.

The decentralization of the administrative power (*pouvoir administratif*), which in fact encompasses the entire sphere of local and regional political life shaped by the citizens themselves, and not by the "administrators," is for Tocqueville one of the chief characteristics of the American union. Since there is no central authority with jurisdiction over local affairs, American citizens themselves take their problems in hand. The communal bodies are structures for self-government of communities and counties. The result is that in the United States political consciousness is widely spread: "the country" is "from the village to the whole Union an object of loving care," for the Americans feel that public affairs are their affairs through dealing with them.

Local politics in this sense, which presupposes that they will be determined, delimited, and guided by the affected citizens of the locality, and not by a central authority, cannot be compared with the "communal self-administration" of the continental European type.

Adolf Gasser rightly points out that the freedom of communities Tocqueville describes is qualitatively different from most of our European local self-administration, which is basically only a matter of "letting distinguished incumbents share in administering in the lowest levels of the governmental system and saturating them as 'honorary officials' with a mentality of bureaucratic subordination."[62] The free community of the kind that Tocqueville learned to know and admire in America as "the people's schools of liberty" and as models for any democratic system is a political unit, which—in principle competent for everything—cedes matters of regional or superregional extent, but settles all questions of the local area and local community itself and on its own responsibility.

Local self-government by citizens in a free community ensures the freedom of the citizens to act in common with other citizens, to confer publicly with each other on their own affairs and to settle them. Its aim is to shape local living conditions and not just to fill areas that the central authorities have left vacant and that the latter steadily restrict by public subsidies and by technical and legal supervision of communal administration, their instruments of manipulation.

The practice of political freedom through local self-government described here should also not be confused with what is termed "participation" in present-day social science literature. Nowadays, for almost all writers using this expression, "participation" signifies general participation in a very markedly centralized process of opinion formation, decision, and planning slanted toward uniformity. The "participation" of the citizens is restricted to feeding their own ideas, interests, and desires into a process leading to the formulation of a uniform concept of all participants. That one cannot call this acting by individual citizens is quite as clear as the result; the participants, who can perceive no direct consequences of actions ultimately attributable to them, cannot develop a consciousness of their responsibility. Also, it is obvious that there is a lot of wishful thinking in the numerous Marxist, Liberal, Social-Democratic, or planification "models" of participation. The citizens are indeed to be brought in; but they are to remain little wheels in a process whose omnipotence they accept perhaps all the more willingly because of their own "participation." This manner of letting citizens participate in planning processes reduces the participants to what the model-makers continually maintain they are: individuals guided only by their own interests. The reason for this is apparent. Why should one be concerned with the desires, ideas, and interests of other citizens if one has no chance really to formulate a particular policy, but only influences it slightly? Participatory models of this kind cannot induce a sense of responsibility for the whole entity, since they do not endow the participants with any responsibility for the whole. And—entirely aside from the most naive models, which as in physics mechanically expect the birth of a common interest from a parallelogram of interest vector forces—they usually let the cat out of the bag in the end: it is the social engineer who tots up the varying interests and produces the common solution, and make-work jobs for the social technicians trained by the model-makers. This kind of "participation" is little more than bureaucracy moderated, possibly curbed, by citizens' input.

In the paradigm of the republic in which the citizens themselves take charge of their own affairs in the local public sphere without centralized administration, power is distributed throughout the whole land. Power is not concentrated in the "state," but resides in the citizens whenever they assemble in joint conference. This kind of power "corresponds to the ability, not just to act but to act in concert."[63]

It is incontestable that this concept, according to which power lies in the communities of citizens, is somewhat qualitatively different from the concept of power which was handed down to most of the modern social sciences from the authoritarian state tradition of Europe.[64] And when Max Weber defines power as "seizing every opportunity within a social relationship to impose one's will, even against opposition, regardless of how the opportunity arises,"[65] he stands in the tradition of centralistic princely sovereignty, as formulated by Thomas Hobbes.

Hobbes is not concerned with democratic gatherings of free and equal citizens, but with the security of the single individual, which is guaranteed by power. "Power is . . .

good, because it is useful for protection; and protection provides security. If it be not extraordinary, it is useless; for what all others have equally is nothing."[66] A person like Hobbes, dominated by fear of death and desire for self-preservation,[67] and hence by mistrust of his fellow citizens, can hardly understand the different character of democratic power in a community of citizens. In Hobbes's *Leviathan* we read that the greatest human power is "that which is compounded of the Powers of most men, united by consent in one person, Naturall, or Civill, that has the use of all their Powers depending on his will; such as is the Power of a Commonwealth."[68] According to this, concentration is the special quality of the kind of power exercised over others. The less citizens have of this kind of power, the greater it is. Power is conveyed as a commodity, is lost to the conveyor, and is exercised by the ruler in the name of the citizens. Thus, the more isolated the individuals who confront him, the stronger the ruler. In this line of reasoning, the accumulation of power in the central government, and not the citizens' capacity to act, becomes the criterion of the power of society. It follows that society is stronger the less the collective individuals in a territory themselves possess the right of decision making. Thus, the prerequisite of power in a commonwealth, paradoxically, would be total lack of structure in society and total impotence of the citizens. A political constitution that preserves the capacity of citizens to act by renouncing centralization is, according to this concept, a nullity.

And Tocqueville prizes precisely this "nullity" as a model. The American republics federated in the union represent in his eyes the successful combination of democratic equality, republican liberty, and the necessary stability. This establishment was successful in large part because of special historical, sociological, and geographical conditions which favored it. But the true achievement of the American union is the utilization of the favorable circumstances, the creation of a responsible, self-confident, and freedom-loving citizen, who feels the republican system is his and practices it, and whose civic spirit—

enhanced by institutions and practice—actively preserves practical freedom in a continuous process of self-education in society.

The mixed constitution

But the degree of freedom given the citizens by the rule of the majority can, for its part, easily lead to a danger to freedom. The will of the majority does not always coincide with justice. The sentiments and opinions of citizens can be vacillating and erratic, and the readiness of many citizens to observe the legal forms that ensure the rights of minorities and single citizens, is not always clear-cut. This means that the rule of the majority does not always automatically guarantee right, justice, and freedom for all citizens, and Tocqueville never tires of depicting the dangers of a majority rule that assumes all powers of decision as a "tyranny of the majority."[69] The unhindered power of a class, group, or person is always an evil. "It seems to me that unlimited power is a bad and dangerous thing. Its exercise appears to me to be beyond the competence of man, whoever he may be, and I see only God who can be omnipotent without danger, because His wisdom and His justice are always equal to His power."[70]

However, Tocqueville rightly recognizes that the mechanistic concept which opines that one could give equal decision-making authority to two or more different bodies within a single sphere, or that one could establish and apply aristocratic and democratic constitutional principles simultaneously and equally in a single sphere of decision making is a "chimera."[71] He explicitly rejects this concept of a mixed constitution. Yet this does not signify that one cannot counterbalance a dominant power, the majority of citizens (in this instance in the United States of America), and a dominant constitutional principle, the democratic rule of the majority, with restraints, brakes, and delaying counterweights.

The American founding fathers recognized this, knew "that a certain authority above the body of the people was necessary, which should enjoy a degree of independence in its sphere without being entirely beyond the popular control; an authority which would be forced to comply with the *permanent* determinations of the majority, but which would be able to resist its caprices and refuse its most dangerous demands."[72] The quasi-monarchical power of the president of the United States, indeed, was subject in part to the will of the majority through the risk of re-election. His veto power and his authority in foreign affairs, however, put him in a position to work against the ups and downs of popular sentiment.

Aside from this, Tocqueville notes the quasi-aristocratic status of American judges and attorneys, whose preference for order, stability, and legal forms make them important bearers of a supervisory power *vis-à-vis* vacillations in moods and passions of the people.[73] Their training, their special status as a corporate body, and their sense of the essence of traditions, oriented to Anglo-Saxon case law based on precedent, gave the legal profession the position of a political establishment moderating popular sentiment. But since these jurists were not an isolated caste and in many political legal cases, in cases of constitutionality, and, especially as presiding judges and directors of procedure, in jury trials had constant exchanges of opinion with society, whose members they were, they could influence the thinking, action, and conduct of their fellow citizens in numerous ways. This is of greatest importance for freedom, for "the sense of justice and the peaceful and lawful intervention of the judge in the sphere of politics is perhaps the most outstanding characteristic of a free people."[74]

Prudence

We have already demonstrated that Tocqueville perceived a decisive advantage in local republican politics in that they attach the habitudes and manner of behavior of the citizens as well as their thinking to freedom. Joint discussion by the citizens of common matters and problems of interest works against the differing ideas of individual groups,[75] clarifies the common cause, and causes the citizens to identify themselves with their republic.[76]

Over and beyond the spirit of freedom, the experience of practical politics engenders in the citizens a kind of political prudence that consists not in knowledge of general laws but rather in the ability to deal with practical situations. Jack Lively notes that Tocqueville had less trust in formal education than John Stuart Mill. "Political education in its broadest sense was essential—he constantly referred to local governments, voluntary associations, juries as 'schools.' "[77]

This practical prudence, acquired through custom, experience, and action, is one of the most important pillars of stability of a democratic republic. It kept American citizens from falling prey to general theoretical propositions, such as those propounded by the philosophers of the eighteenth century, whose stormy passions were not moderated by experience.[78]

The local political institutions of the union are thus considerable educational factors that teach citizens to look into details and so to recognize the weaknesses of generalized theories. "If, then, there is a subject upon which a democratic people is peculiarly liable to abandon itself, blindly and extravagantly, to general ideas, the best corrective that can be used will be to make that subject a part of their daily practical occupation. They will then be compelled to enter into details, and the details will teach them the weak points of the theory. This remedy may frequently be a painful one, but its effect is certain."[79]

It is precisely because in democracies there is a tendency toward general concepts and a certain contempt for concrete details that this "practical prudence"[80] is important, for "if the Americans had not been gradually accustomed to govern themselves, their book-learning would not help much at the present day."[81]

What Tocqueville asserts here is completely contradictory to the present-day intellectual climate enamored of general theory. Michael Oakeshott's work on *Rationalism in Politics* points out the alienation from reality caused by generalized theories and stresses the particular value of education through experience.[82] Tocqueville does exactly the same, putting book-learning to one side as something different in character from the experience of the practitioner. So he presents us with the concept of a citizen who through practical acquaintance with the law and guided by an attorney acquires a sense of justice and adherence to legal form, and through public cooperation gains experience in political freedom, begins to love freedom, and by solving concrete problems acquires the practical prudence that binds him to the real world into which he was born.

Hence, the multifariousness of reality in a republic, its laws, the sphere of public action, and the sphere of practical problems bound up with the laws have their parallels in citizens who make tangible the virtues essential for the life of the republic through custom and judgment. In this manner, the correspondence of the citizens' political virtues and the social system stabilizes order in a republic, which tends to be unstable.

THE INTELLECTUAL AND SPIRITUAL FOUNDATION OF VIRTUE

Self-interest

The love of freedom and the habituation into the advantages of freedom, gained through practice, which distinguish citizens in a democratic republic, are not always sufficient to provide that degree of stability to the system which guarantees freedom in a republic. Tocqueville knows that people weigh, calculate, ponder anything of value to them. This means that the pragmatic, calculating reason of the citizens must be won over to the blessings of freedom and its virtues. In the union of the United States of America, this occurs through the precept of enlightened self-interest.

Tocqueville observed in America a fundament of virtuous conduct which was, to him, peculiar and new: "In the United States one does not say that virtue is good. One makes sure that it is useful, and proves it daily. . . . Hence, the American moralists . . . do not argue against the fact that everyone pursues his own advantage, but they diligently insist that virtue is advantageous for everyone."[83] The precept of enlightened self-interest, which to Tocqueville "seems best suited in all the philosophical teachings to the needs of mankind in our time,"[84] should not be confused with the flat assertion, spread abroad by Adam Smith's economic doctrine of the invisible hand, that everyone who pursues his own advantage in the end serves the common welfare by his actions.[85] Rather, Tocqueville's argumentation is based on virtuous action and teaches that this is beneficial. It does not fail to expound virtues, but demonstrates the benefits of virtue, having due regard to the pressure on the human mind "to seek benefits." In order for the citizen to understand this precept, he must have a great amount of knowledge and learning; but he will then be able to perceive that it contains such a large number of illuminating truths that people can live according to it.

Religion

Despite the great advantages offered by the precept of enlightened self-interest, it may not completely guide people in their spiritual existence toward virtuous actions in a republic. "No matter how much one strives to realize the utility of virtue, it will always be difficult for a person who does not wish to die, to lead a just life."[86] With this observation, Tocqueville reaches a consideration that brushes aside all reflections on utility—the mortality of man. The fact that human life takes place between birth and death, that man is mortal, that he nevertheless carries out actions in particular situations whose meaning lies beyond his organic existence demonstrates that man's consciousness can transcend death. Some things are more important than preserving one's own life. Whatever may be the particular symbolic expressions of this experience, that there is something set above life, with this observation Tocqueville advances into a realm relating to the connection between man and the divine, to the transcendence of the human mind over and beyond its organic existence, that is, religion.

It is important to note how Tocqueville addresses the question of religion. He is interested first of all in the contribution that religion—the Christian faith in the case of the United States of America and Catholicism in the case of France—can make to the growth, maintenance, and stabilization of a free society. The issue raised by Tocqueville as to the significance of religion for a republic confronts Christianity and Catholicism with a problem that does not lie at the center of theological or religious considerations concerning Christian existence in society. According to such considerations, political freedom and republican order may be important *desiderata* for a Christian, which help to make life in this world more bearable, but they are of secondary significance for Christian existence under God.

In other words, Tocqueville poses his questions regarding Christianity and Catholicism "from outside"; it is not a matter of a Catholic Christian being moved by the question of the compatibility and the reciprocal value of faith and political freedom, but instead a republican is inquiring into the value of religion for a free system. This explains the peculiar, almost technical coldness with which Tocqueville treats the problems concerned. He declared in a letter to Arthur de Gobineau that he was not a believer, and in fact Tocqueville was alienated from Catholicism.[87]

It is well-known and convincingly demonstrated in the work of Doris Goldstein,[88] that the encounter of young Alexis with Enlightenment literature of the eighteenth century in his father's library at Metz gave a death blow to his faith, presumably maintained till then by sheltering from the laicist outer world. The destruction of his faith presumably held in his youth in the form of pious rites and dogma must surely be blamed on the desolate condition of milieu-theology of the nineteenth century, which only taught the evasion of the existential tension of Christian existence under God by certitudes and articles of dogma.[89] And the efforts of his teacher and fatherly friend, Lesueur, to keep him from "bad influences"[90] testify more to the family priest's love than to a well-planned education that would have prepared the young man for the atmosphere of Enlightenment in French society.

Although this explanation may satisfy the biographer, Tocqueville's continual preoccupation with questions regarding religion shows very clearly that for him the problem was not at all "solved." On the contrary, Tocqueville's seeming aloofness from the essence of faith and religiosity is only the surface masking his suffering from loss of faith. His wrestling with the questions of religion and faith led to problems that are typical for the tension affecting the modern enlightened and liberal citizen, who does not shove aside the relationship of religion, politics, and society with the trite slogan that religion is a private matter.

His reflections on stability and freedom in political societies made him realize that a society without religion is threatened with anarchy or despotism. His observations of men, and thereby himself, led him to the conclusion that men have a personal "urgent need" for religion; and his reflections on political freedom caused him to doubt "that man can ever bear complete independence from religion and complete political freedom."[91]

It thus appears that Tocqueville recognized fully that complete irreligiosity frees impulses in the human psyche, especially in a free society, which threaten order, stability, and freedom, and he repeatedly insists on the wholesome influence of religion, which teaches overconfident human reason its limits.[92]

But after all, it is not immediately self-evident that human reason needs the "wholesome yoke" of religion, at least not in the spiritual environment shaped by the eighteenth century *"philosophes"*[93] which also influenced Tocqueville. Tocqueville, however, carefully avoids drawing the conclusion implicit in his desire to make men aware of the limitations on their insight despite all intellectual searching for perfection. He presents no interpretation of human existence between God and animals, he articulates no explanation of human nature that looks upon men as "under God" and interprets their spiritual searching for perfection as a movement toward God. Caught in an intellectual milieu that viewed faith as a phenomenon which God implants in men's hearts by "supernatural means," or as a consequence of men's "longing for immortality," as an answer to the "urgent needs" of men,[94] he retreats to a position concerned only with the effects of religious feeling for a republic and freedom. "I am at this moment considering religions in a purely human point of view; my object is to inquire by what means they may most easily retain their sway in the democratic ages upon which we are entering."[95] These words from *Democracy in America* are astonishing. A man who has lost faith himself is concerned to preserve the dominion of religion. Why does Tocqueville, irreligious himself, wish to preserve the dominion of religion?

The peculiarity of Tocqueville's desire seems even stranger, when one remembers that by dominion of religion he does not mean direct political influence of the churches. Not only in his books, but also in his speeches in parliament Tocqueville pleaded for separation of Church and State. This very separation is for him the prerequisite for preserving the dominion of religion, which is to be accomplished through influence on the faithful and not through an alliance with the rulers harmful to the Church. Hence, Tocqueville hopes to ensure the dominion of religion through a faith he does not share. What exactly is this dominion?

First of all, Christianity has a moral objective. It should make clear the limits of human action in the consciousness of citizens. The unhindered dominion of Christianity brings it about "that every principle of the moral world is fixed and determinate," and this is precisely necessary where "the political world is abandoned to the debates and experiments of men." The impassable limits of human existence are in this manner observed.[96] The spiritual modesty taught by religion is obviously to restrain men from overestimating themselves and from self-idolatry, which Tocqueville criticizes in the French thinkers of the eighteenth century. In actual fact, the *philosophes* worshipped not so much human reason as their own. "No one ever manifested less confidence than those men in the wisdom of the masses," who displayed not only contempt for the common man, but "the pride of rivals" toward God.[97]

The result of this hybrid attitude was a "boundless confidence" in their own reason, which granted these men the ability to rearrange laws, institutions, and morals as they wished.[98] This cast of mind, which claims that everything is at the disposition of human action and human reason finally results in the government taking "the place of providence" in the citizens' consciousness.[99]

If people believe they can, guided and coordinated in their actions by a government, shape *everything* as they wish, they convince themselves in fact that the first incomplete Creation can be corrected by a second one made by human hands. Tocqueville perceives that the power allowed in this fantasy of "freedom" to the seemingly omnipotent government which will supposedly realize these dreams leads to the invention of new forms of slavery.[100]

Thus, Tocqueville initially displays an understanding of the possible results of the metaphysical revolt for politics and assigns to religion the task of preventing them by spreading faith. Yet he does not pursue further the philosophical-theoretical scope of man's self-idolatry.

His attention concentrated on the tasks of religion for freedom, he turns to the effects of religion on the practical actions of men in society. For Tocqueville it is primarily, apparently even exclusively, a matter of the usefulness that a generally accepted religion has for society. Symbols and claims to truth are not the subject of his attention. He declares quite reservedly that while the truth of faith is of great importance to the individual, this is not the case for society. "Society has no future life to hope for or to fear; and provided the citizens profess a religion, the peculiar tenets of that religion are of little importance to its interests."[101] This means that the results of faith are apparently his sole object of investigation.

These results, however, are very useful for society. It is religion that teaches people that there is something more important than life, and this is necessary, "for one finds it very difficult to preach to people that one must die for virtue, if one believes that they really will die."[102] In other words, religion takes people out of their everyday triviality;[103] it can give people the consciousness of the purpose of their existence that makes them capable of practicing civic-political virtues going beyond actions based on rightly understood self-interest.[104] Thereby it is a considerable ally of a republic in the struggle against that dangerous evil of the democratic spirit, individualism,[105] which permits the citizen to live as if he owes nothing to society. The typically intelligent American pastor does not oppose individualism and the pursuit of prosperity; he links them together and works to see that these passions do not dominate the citizens entirely; thus enough room remains for political activities *and* regard and care for neighbors, the parish, the community, and society.[106]

Religion accustoms people to make concessions to higher goals. In addition to this function, it is a common bond in everyday life, which binds citizens together and unites them. Besides patriotism, only religion can "long urge all the people towards the same end."[107]

The "very simple ideas"

With a superficial reading of this high praise of the useful influence of religiosity one could easily get the impression that Tocqueville's reflections are simply the cynical strategies of a nonbeliever, who tries to condition his fellow citizens by pious myths to a useful way of life in a republic. Yet the problem is not so simple. Tocqueville is most certainly not a devout Catholic; but he is anything but irreligious. The precepts he wishes the Church to teach, he holds to be true and right.

In a letter to Bouchitté of 1858, he wrote that he never proceeded very far with his philosophical studies, but that there was a small number of very simple ideas. "These ideas lead easily to belief in a First Cause, which remains both evident and insufficient; in fixed laws, shown in the physical world, which one must impute to the moral world; in the Providence of God and consequently in His justice; in the responsibility of man for his actions, who can distinguish between good and evil, and therefore to belief in another life. . . ."[108]

It is striking that his "philosophical faith" has a direct relation to the sphere of actions and man's responsibility for what he does or fails to do. Concerning God, whose justice he never doubts,[109] his intimations are very guarded. It seems as if they are only set forth to justify his confidence in future developments. In the same letter to Bouchitté, Tocqueville writes of the "basis which I will not touch on" and means the "basis for the existence of the world . . . the plan of this Creation, of which we know nothing, not even of our body and still less of our mind."

But trust in God without certitude and without rest for the soul drives Tocqueville to an intellectual grappling with the things of this world. His soul, he writes to Beaumont, is ill at ease in his body and therefore seeks the activity of great intellectual endeavors. This restlessness of the quest, the consequence of unrest of the soul, is the motor pushing him to labor. If he had ever found rest for his mind and soul, he would probably not have applied his mind to mental efforts. For these efforts to reach peace of mind "are so painful for me, that if I could only tolerably achieve peace of mind, I would certainly never emerge again."[110]

It appears that Tocqueville consciously or unconsciously pushes the philosophical-theoretical questions aside, to make room for the realm of political activity interesting him. His interest lies in the world of men. He turns to it, away from spiritual questions. "Enough of this matter," he writes at the end of a long passage on religion in a letter to Louis de Kergorlay, ". . . if I plunged into it often, it would drive me crazy,"[111] in order to turn back to pragmatic political questions. Tocqueville displays a strong tendency to reduce religious and spiritual questions to acceptance or rejection of dogmas,[112] and so to set them aside. But in any case, he seems to have the fixed conviction that religion can be effective for the mass of people only in the form of dogmatic statements. This is also the reason, in his opinion, that these "very simple ideas" resulting from a painful process of reflection, which lead through faith from doubt to conviction,[113] are ill suited as religious teaching for the people. Most people simply do not have the leisure to subject themselves to the process of reflection leading to these insights—entirely aside from the fact that such investigation far exceeds the average abilities of men.[114] Above all, these "very simple ideas" do not convey that degree of assurance and certainty gained by recognition of one authority in dogmatic questions, and this assurance Tocqueville holds to be urgently necessary.

To state Tocqueville's problem with religiosity in radical terms: there is a tense relationship between the content of faith, as formulated by Tocqueville in the "very simple ideas," and the necessity to propagate, spread, and anchor faith in the people, which is required for the sake of the republic. Taking note of this tense relationship helps to explain several of Tocqueville's formulations in his discussions of religion that would otherwise be inexplicable: thus, when he believes he can present a basis for religion by arguments concerning the usefulness of religion,[115] or when he speaks of the position of the doubter (doubtless explaining his own situation), who can no longer believe, but hides this from his compatriots.[116] Even Tocqueville's portrayal of the widespread and assured status of faith in the United States is obviously written with the intent to teach; in a lengthy letter to Louis de Kergorlay he wrote of the indolence of faith and general indifference of the Americans.[117]

"*Pascal said: To be mistaken in believing that the Christian religion is true is no great loss to anyone; but how dreadful to be mistaken in believing it to be false.*"[118]

The tense relationship noted above between the "very simple ideas" and the necessity to propagate religion for the sake of

the republic led Tocqueville—in search for unity in the republic to maintain its order, it must be emphasized—to a most
peculiar attempt to solve the evident problem. Tocqueville
seriously considered the possibility of a special religion for
the educated dominant classes, who would yet be associated
with their fellow citizens in the practice of the cult.

It cannot be ignored that the "very simple ideas" noted
above in the letter to Bouchitté are conceptions "of God, of
his relations with the human race, of the nature of their souls,
and their duties to each other."[119] After the aforementioned
reference to the impossibility of philosophical reflection for
most citizens, Tocqueville at once stresses the stark necessity
of fixed dogmatic articles of faith grounded on authority, and
bases this necessity on the faculty of religion to direct the
cravings of people to goals beyond material enjoyment.[120]
This faculty of religion is so important for Tocqueville that
he seems to think it justifiable to recommend that the representatives and intellectual leaders of society should show
adherence to the prevailing religion, even though they do
not actually share all the articles of faith.

There are a number of indications that the ideas Tocqueville
develops in the chapter "How Religion In The United States
Avails Itself Of Democratic Tendencies" were first formulated in a letter to his close friend Louis de Kergorlay of 29
June 1831[121] and that he used this letter in setting down the
chapter.[122] But in the letter Tocqueville formulated ideas
which did not appear in *Democracy in America*. He writes:
"Will deism ever be right for all classes of a nation? Especially
for those who need the reins of religion. I am not at all convinced of it. I grant that what I see here inclines me more than
before to believe that what one calls natural religion is sufficient for the upper classes, provided that the faith in the two
or three great truths it teaches is real, and provided that something of an outward worship mixes and visibly unites people
in their public profession of these truths; but either the people
will become different from what it ever was and still is in all

parts of the world, or it will see nothing else in this religion than the absence of any faith in an after-life and consequently will fall headlong into the doctrine of selfish interest." Then Tocqueville emphasizes that this is only a tendency, that Americans in fact think more highly of morals than do the French, only to say in wonder and regret that there is only one religion which truly completely absorbs the consciousness of men, but which divides mankind into believers and the damned, and produces intolerance and fanaticism. Aside from this there is natural religion; "it preaches tolerance, joins itself to reason and makes that its symbol; it has no power of any sort; it is a motionless object without strength and almost lifeless." These last observations make apparent at least a degree of sympathy for natural religion on Tocqueville's part. Yet, at the same time, he knows that deism does not really seize people with religious faith, which he considers so essential. The fact that Tocqueville did not reveal these considerations to the readers of *Democracy in America*[123] seems to me to be proof of his attitude, which is that the truth of the symbolic interpretation of man's realization of his existence under God is secondary compared to the understanding of the necessity of religion for the citizens for the sake of the free republic.

With Tocqueville, however, this retreat from the problems of religion leads, at least by implication, to regarding religion from the viewpoint of its effects on the more important republic. For the sake of unity in freedom Tocqueville only hints at the question of a special religion for the intellectual leading classes; otherwise the propagation of freedom might suffer.

This last thought seems to me to be one Tocqueville refrained from pursuing, but is hinted at in *The Old Regime* and correspondence with Gobineau. Tocqueville was very conscious of the tension between the supranational ecumenical religion of Christianity and the organizational form of the nation-state. In *Democracy in America* he formulated the relation between religion and political society in Augustinian terms. "If the human mind be left to follow its own bent, it will regulate the temporal and spiritual institutions of society in a uniform manner, and man will endeavor, if I may so speak, to *harmonize* earth with heaven."[124]

Since Christianity in principle addresses all people, it incurs a tense relationship with political entities organized on specific territories and particular populations such as the nation-state of the nineteenth century. Christ interpreted His existence under God with symbols valid for all mankind. The City of God, with which Christians accordingly align their concepts of political society, explodes the categories of the nation-state, which cannot be the highest element of order. The heathen religions of antiquity, in contrast, "which were all more or less combined with the political constitution or the social order of a nation, and maintained even in their dogmas a certain national physiognomy, often of a city, normally remained within the limits of a territory from which they hardly ever spread. . . ." They therefore were never directed by evangelical zeal,[125] which characterizes Christianity. So the problem arises that Christianity with its worldwide claim is poorly suited to define the duties and virtues of the citizen *vis-à-vis* his fatherland.[126] The development of an order rising above that of the nation-state is one possible outcome; deviations into imperialism and un-Christian idolatry of the national power-state, including its expansion, can also be the consequences of the unresolved tension between ecumenical Christianity and organization on national political lines. The nineteenth century, and Tocqueville, too, took this second path, because he did not think this problem through to the end. Nationalism, which Tocqueville at least in one passage equated with the Christian religion because they both promote social unity,[127] converts into imperialism and colonialism. The desire to extend European civilization legitimized aggressive expansion of national territory and oppression of other people with the aim to civilize.

Individualism, pursuit of wealth, and despotism

The successful special instance of the American union, as depicted by Tocqueville, is not the sole and central subject of his interest. From his book and from a number of letters we have shown that he makes clear he is concerned with France. What is suggested by a few intimations in the first part of *Democracy in America* in 1835, and especially in historical digressions, becomes in the second part (1840) the central point of his reflections: the threats to freedom in French democracy. In *The Old Regime, Recollections,* also in unpublished studies of Great Britain and India, and in many notes and letters, Tocqueville severely criticizes societies that have fallen into disorder. He describes the threats to freedom in his fatherland and develops a critical analysis of French bourgeois society. After 1830, this society was ruled by the mentality of the middle class, "active, industrious, often dishonest, generally orderly, but sometimes rash because of vanity and selfishness, timid by temperament, moderate in all things except a taste for well-being and: mediocre. . . ."[128] The problem was that this mentality of the middle class governed all spheres of society, including politics. "Master of the whole entity . . . the middle class, which one must call the ruling class . . . took on the quality of private entrepreneurship. It entrenched itself in its power, soon afterwards also in its egoism, and all its adherents thought far more of their private businesses than of public affairs, far more of their pleasure than of the grandeur of the nation. Posterity, which sees only those crimes which leap to the eye, and generally overlooks vice, will probably never know to what an extent the government at that time assumed the behavior of an economic enterprise, whose activities are determined by the goal of profit for the partners."[129] With these comments Tocqueville did not denounce or morally damn the pursuit of gain or love of material well-being. He only wanted to set it in place in the hierarchy of goals for human activity, which does not set affluence as the highest and all-determining goal. What Tocqueville criticizes is not the existence of the passion for gaining wealth; he knows that no society with dispassionate angels as citizens could serve as the premise for a critique of actual contemporary conditions. Rather, his criticism is directed against the fact that pursuit of wealth had completely excluded every other goal. "I do not reproach equality for the fact that it drives men to chase after forbidden pleasures, but for the fact that it completely obsesses them with the pursuit of permitted pleasures. By these means a kind of virtuous materialism may ultimately be established in the world, which would not corrupt, but enervate, the soul and noiselessly unbend its springs of action."[130] The criticism is directed against the complete saturation of society by the thought of gain, which subordinates all virtues to reckoning expense and gain, and which makes individual advantage the citizens' guiding rule and society's dominant principle.

The prerequisite of this development was the depoliticization of society, whereby the citizens no longer experienced political activity, as all powers of decision were gathered into the central government. The citizens withdrew into their own private affairs and were connected with politics solely through their own interests, which brought them into politics.

Tocqueville developed the symbol of "individualism" for the way of life of withdrawal from the community and the citizens' self-restriction to the private sphere as follows: "Individualism is a mature and calm feeling, which disposes each member of the community to sever himself from the mass of his fellows and to draw apart with his family and his friends, so that after he has thus formed a little circle of his own, he willingly leaves society at large to itself. . . . Individualism proceeds from erroneous judgment more than from depraved feelings; it originates as much in deficiencies of mind as in perversity of heart . . . individualism, at first, only saps the virtues of public life; but in the long run it attacks and destroys all others and is at length absorbed in downright selfishness."¹³¹ Individualism, destructive of the political citizen's virtue, the withdrawal into private existence, the "retirement from society" (in Jürgen Gebhardt's phrase), is one of the greatest dangers confronting democratic societies.¹³² The danger is particularly great for democracies, because neither traditions of other conduct nor the existence of a special political class, the aristocracy, oppose individualism's effective penetration of society. This "absolutization of the bourgeois"¹³³ is for Tocqueville the chief danger in the general development toward equal living conditions, causing men to forget how much they actually are interdependent. It leads the bourgeois "continually back to himself alone and threatens to immure him in the end in the loneliness of his own heart."¹³⁴

This individualistic way of life produces a type of citizen who secludes himself with his family and friends, and creates "for himself a small society for his own needs." He begins to imagine that his whole fate is in his own hands.¹³⁵

Naturally, this type is not new. It is the *idiotes* known already to Plato and Aristotle, the private man who thinks he has nothing to do with politics and society. What is new here, what Tocqueville sets forth, is not so much the existence of this way of life, as its dominance in modern democracy, spreading from the middle class to encompass all classes of society. There are two plausible causes for this:

1. Owing to the prospective equality of conditions the citizens are no longer held together, as in nations ruled by aristocracies, by a host of duties, obligations, and legal relations of a specific kind, determined by tradition. One "owes nothing to anyone."¹³⁶

2. In a democracy, new ways are opened for those who had no chance to advance or no possibilities to amass property, ways that they quickly perceive. And these new possibilities of advancement and wealth threaten to cast their spell so strongly on the majority of citizens that they render the economic reality of society decisive and enfold all its activities within this sphere. The private pursuit of prosperity becomes the decisive motive in acting to which all else is subordinated.

Hence, economic interest becomes the common goal uniting all private persons in society, who are otherwise withdrawn into individualism.

What the prerevolutionary society could hardly offer—namely, advancement and acquisition of property—became the sole worthwhile activity for the middle class, which largely determined the intellectual atmosphere and maxims of conduct. The old regime established on feudal principles and according to classes entailed unequal division of property and comfort. And individuals had no opportunity to alter their economic status. "In aristocratic communities the wealthy, never having experienced a condition different from their own, entertain no fear of changing it; the existence of such conditions hardly occurs to them. The comforts of life are not to them the end of life, but simply a way of living; they regard them as existence itself, enjoyed but scarcely thought of. . . ." Through this privileged status members of the aristocracy are enabled to devote themselves to things other than material, economic goals. "In a nation where aristocracy predominates in society and keeps it stationary, the people in the end get as much accustomed to poverty as the rich to their opulence. The latter bestow no anxiety on their physical comforts because they enjoy them without an effort; the former do not think of things which they despair of obtaining. . . . When, on the contrary, the distinctions of ranks are obliterated and privileges are destroyed, when hereditary property is subdivided and education and freedom are widely diffused, the desire of acquiring the comforts of the world haunts the imagination of the poor, and the dread of losing them that of the rich. Many scanty fortunes spring up; those who possess them have a sufficient share of physical gratifications to conceive a taste for these pleasures, but not enough to satisfy it. . . . If I were to inquire what passion is most natural to men who are stimulated and circumscribed by the obscurity of their birth or the mediocrity of their fortune, I could discover none more peculiarly appropriate to their condition than this love of physical prosperity. The passion for physical comforts is essentially a passion of the middle classes; with those classes it grows and spreads, with them it is preponderant. From them it mounts into the higher orders of society and descends into the mass of the people."[137]

For Tocqueville, one of the causes of dangers to political freedom is that passion, the pursuit of comfort, employed in modern economic theories for the interpretation of nearly all human behavior.[138] Concerning men in prerevolutionary France, he wrote that they "had little of that passion for material well-being which breeds servitude, debilitating yet tenacious and unchanging, which willingly mixes and intertwines itself, so to speak, in various private virtues. . . . It allows rectitude and forbids heroism, and excels in making well-behaved people and cowardly citizens."[139] Cowardly citizens, who neither love nor defend their freedom, but misuse it only for private acquisition of wealth, and leave politics either to the central authorities, or make it an instrument of gaining wealth, are for Tocqueville the greatest danger for a free republic. Wherever, owing to the dominance of the pursuit of wealth, economic calculations rule, rather than the love of freedom, free republican institutions become only a hollow shell. Tocqueville perceived this hollowness as a general corruption in French society and knew it could lead to destruction of the republic. He interpreted this phenomenon observed in France as a general problem for democracy and as a structural danger for a democratic republic.

Politics and economics

The pursuit of comfort released by equality of conditions and the resulting individualism had to be moderated by the spiritual, intellectual, habitual, and institutional training of the citizens directed toward freedom, and directed into ways promoting freedom. The presentation of this goal shows once again the priority Tocqueville gives to political freedom. His insistence on the priority of freedom over the pursuit of comfort signifies the priority of politics over economics in which freedom is set above the upper level of values. Political freedom is the prerequisite for pursuit of comfort and riches and not vice versa, as conventionally claimed in recent times usually without dispute.

There were examples in history of nations governed as republics in which were neither craftsmen nor merchants, Tocqueville noted in England in 1835, "but I perceive no nation of craftsmen or merchants which was not free. . . . There is therefore a hidden relation between *freedom and commerce*. . . . I think it is the spirit and customs of freedom which produce the spirit and customs of commerce."[140] In order to be free, one must be accustomed to developing his own initiatives; one must be able to withstand difficult situations; and one must become accustomed to lead an exciting, active, and dangerous life, always alert to remain master of the situation. The habit so developed in the free citizen does not differ in principle from the qualities and manner of behavior that characterize a successful businessman,[141] although his actions are directed toward other goals.

So it is not astonishing that a system which ensures freedoms to the citizens and affords them opportunities for responsible activities is a precondition for a society to attain economic wealth. Political freedom sets free forces in society that promote its affluence, which is due less to material conditions, mineral deposits, for example, than to the inner strength of a nation.[142] But one must be careful not "to confuse freedom with some of the results it produces." It is not identical with earning money.[143]

The growing wealth gained by the pursuit of comfort and based on the republican order, which fosters the virtues of self-initiative, independence, and the joy of taking the initiative in society, actually threatens to stop up its own source. The child, pursuit of comfort, threatens to eat up its father, the love of freedom. This threat betokens "a most dangerous passage in the history of a democratic people."[144] If the practice of freedom is not yet axiomatic, a society on the way to equality succumbs to conditions "outside it"; its citizens devote themselves only to the pursuit of prosperity and neglect freedom. Possessed by the desire for affluence, they feel burdened by the practice of freedom and the trouble associated with it, all too easily look upon every disturbance of their acquisitiveness as anarchy, "and are always ready to give up freedom at the first disorder."[145] A person who does not know that "to those who know how to retain it, freedom in the long run brings comfort and well-being,"[146] but that wealth and freedom are not the same, will endanger wealth for failing to be concerned with freedom. And the experiences a nation undergoes while wealth grows harbor the tendency to nurture this process of destroying freedom for the sake of comfort. This love of economic prosperity guides men "mainly . . . into business and manufactures. Although these pursuits often bring about great commotions and disasters, they cannot prosper without strictly regulated habits and a long routine of petty uniform acts,"[147] that is, industrial production based on the destruction of handicraft skills by division of labor. People improve themselves through the dexterity of small manipulations by which they earn their bread. But in doing so they are seduced into neglect of their intellectual abilities. Bringing Adam Smith's famous economic example back to real society, Tocqueville asks: "What should one expect from a man who has spent twenty years of his life producing heads for pins?"[148] Tocqueville was vividly aware of the workers' alienation resulting from the industrial labor system.[149] But, unlike his famous contemporary (Marx), he was not possessed by a faith in a final revolution and its consequent solution, and therefore investigated the consequences of this alienation for politics, society, and stable order.

The workers, trained only in a small sphere of activity, intellectually ruined, were being chained to their workplaces and falling more and more into dependence on the entrepreneur,[150] who, for his part, accepted an ever more varied lifestyle provided by larger profits, expansion of his enterprise, and mental activity.

Tocqueville knew very well that industrial mass production would bring forth a new class distinction in society and, investigating the status of industrialists in the United States of America, asked: "What is this, if not aristocracy?"[151] At the same time, moreover, he recognized that this new "aristocracy of manufacturers" surpassed all previous aristocracies in severity, was unrelated to its employees, and devoid of any obligation to them. "The manufacturer demands from the worker only his work, and the worker expects only his wage. Neither one is obligated to protect or to defend the other, and neither one is bound for long by custom or duty to the other. . . . The landed aristocracy of former ages was either bound by law, or thought itself bound by usage, to come to the relief of its serving-men and to relieve their distresses. But the manufacturing aristocracy of our age first impoverishes and debases the men who serve it and then abandons them to be supported by the charity of the public. . . . Between the workman and the master there are frequent relations, but no real association."[152]

Even though Tocqueville overestimates the effect of economic competition and states that the new aristocracy does not constitute a class, since it is not bound together by common aims, traditions, and hopes,[153] he still perceives other effects resulting from the absence of obligations in relations between manufacturers and workers. The care of workers, especially in crises, is delegated to society and in effect to the central government. "Manufacturers generally collect a multitude of men on the same spot, among whom new and complex relations spring up. These men are exposed by their calling to great and sudden alternations of plenty and want, during which public tranquillity is endangered. It may also happen that these employments sacrifice the health and even the life of those who gain by them or of those who live by them. Thus the manufacturing classes require more regulation, superintendence, and restraint than the other classes of society, and it is natural that the powers of government should increase in the same proportion as those classes."[154] It is obvious that these observations of Tocqueville about industrial production sounded extremely critical. He saw the future of democracy in small enterprises, which he thought would have to pay higher wages and take more interest in their employees,[155] and he judged all of these by agricultural production.

His aversion was mainly due to experience he had with industrialists. "I have insurmountable prejudices against industrial laboring, even against the largest of them. I have spent twelve years of my life with politicians, of whom a great number were also occupied with industrial questions. Also, although there is in some degree an affinity and a certain kinship in these two careers, I have almost found that occupation with industrial questions influenced the feelings and thoughts of those who were concerned with them in a manner which was not good in the long run."[156] And thus Tocqueville recognized that the fixed outlook of the modern citizen in industry, characterized by pursuit of wealth or even of moderate material comfort, is difficult to reconcile with his own concept of active political freedom in a republic. For one thing, the complete domination of the citizen's thinking and actions by the passion for well-being can lead to the autocracy of a tyrant, or to people's representatives who monopolize politics among themselves. Since most people are busy with other things, they gladly leave politics to a few. But it is also possible that the formal framework of the constitution is maintained, that no dictatorship supplants democratic institutions, and yet freedom is lost.

The problem of freedom in society is not solved only by institutional regulations, and hence the dangers of a *coup d'état* and institutional changes are by no means the only ones that threaten freedom. People "obsessed by the passion for material goods" are generally inclined to consider politics and the public unrest it entails as a disturbance of their private life. They are subjects (Tocqueville uses the expression "slaves"), even though there is no autocrat.[157] They are not active as citizens and are easily ruled as a result of their narrow interest in economic activity, if only their economic endeavors are given free rein. These observations of Tocqueville about modern France of his time caused him to modify his statements on the threat of loss of freedom in democracy, while neglecting institutional questions as a problem for the way of life.[158]

Modern "administrative despotism," as he called the new manner of governing after initial hesitation, does not aim at oppressing the citizens. Its apolitical character makes this unnecessary. "When I consider the petty passions of our contemporaries, the mildness of their manners, the extent of their education, the purity of their religion, the gentleness of their morality, their regular and industrious habits, and the restraint which they almost all observe in their vices no less than in their virtues, I have no fear that they will meet with tyrants in their rulers, but rather with guardians."[159]

Tocqueville recognized a completely new kind of servitude, which occurs from the fact that the government holds the citizens in a lifelong absence of responsibility and authority, citizens who willingly subject themselves to this tutelage. A mighty governmental administrative apparatus takes unto itself the cares and problems of the subjects, takes care of them, protects them, guides production and distribution, and deals with all the problems of daily life. "The will of man is not shattered, but softened, bent, and guided; men are seldom forced by it to act, but they are constantly restrained from acting. . . . In this way the nation is reduced to nothing better than a flock of timid and industrious animals, of which the government is the shepherd."[160]

The fact that the nation chooses its own guardians does not alter the servitude; it only renders it more tolerable.[161]

And the guardian government draws more and more authority to itself, centralizes all local decisions, and so causes the citizens, who are losing their custom of dealing with their own affairs themselves, to become ever more markedly dependent on the central authority. Because it is in practice not exercised, the faculty of independent thinking and acting is lost to the citizens. So the burning question is whether these continually degraded private persons, this "nation of servants," is still able to choose effective and wise men for the government.[162] Tocqueville's penetrating description of this mixture of governmental despotism and national sovereignty must not be mistaken for cultural criticism of the tearful, pessimistic conservative sort. It is a cautionary exposition of possible developments on the way to equality, which will threaten society, when in a nation "the taste for physical gratification among them has grown more rapidly than their education and their experience of free institutions."[163] The remedies against these dangers of individualism and pursuit of material comfort are presented by the insights gained from the investigation in America into the beneficial effect of local politics and the practice of freedom. Tocqueville pleads their cause; he describes the desolate condition of France with a therapeutic purpose. The description and criticism are designed to sharpen and win over the mind of the reader to the alternative of the democratic republic.

THE FRENCH REVOLUTION

Tocqueville's exposition of the positive effects of a decentralized political constitution (the penetration of society by practical common sense, the propagation of the public political consciousness, the diffusion of a consensus for political freedom that holds the pursuit of prosperity within limits, the citizens' love of freedom), his emphasis on the political utility of a generally recognized religion, and his description of the beneficial effect of the cooperation of monarchical, aristocratic, and democratic principles are all shaped by his yearning to stabilize political and social relations within the French body politic shaken to pieces by the Revolution. This statement should not lead to the conclusion that Tocqueville was a conservative fanatic for order of the modern type. On the contrary, as we have shown, for him stability and order are not goals in themselves, but worthy goals for the sake of freedom, which is practicable only in orderly relations. The experience of instability in France engendered his quest for an order that would make possible freedom in practice and responsibility of the citizens for themselves.

Tocqueville did not consider the French Revolution to be a chain of events of a few years before and after the storming of the Bastille. Rather, he interpreted it as a political, social, and intellectual process that began long before 1789, came on the political stage with the events of the first years of the Revolution, continued, comprehended the First Republic, the Napoleonic Empire, the Restoration, 1830, the Bourgeois Monarchy, 1848, and the Second Republic, and which had not yet ended with the *coup d'état* of Napoleon III.[164]

Tocqueville's sensitive perception of the fragility of the political systems in which he lived, and his observations on the current revolutionary ideologies and hopes before and after 1848 never led him to hold the view that the Revolution had come to an end. He interpreted French history as a continuing revolutionary process beginning long before 1789, which, interrupted by phases of relative peace and the dictatorship of Napoleon III, had not yet found a perceptible end.[165]

And in fact we recognize even today in the twentieth century that the extent of the process of change worked on modern societies by the American Revolution and ensuing French Revolution cannot be conjectured as to its final conclusion. The transformation in man's understanding of himself in his status in society and history, the revolution in the production process, the complete rearrangement of the social relations of citizens with equal rights among themselves, and the creation of new institutions in the sphere of social relations, the economic system, and the political constitutions are indeed so radical that Hegel's statement that a new epoch began with the French Revolution is fully understandable.

The American and French Revolutions, in fact, called into question one of the most important stabilizing factors in the list of justifications of the legitimacy of political orders: tradition. While through their constitution the Americans succeeded in establishing a new basis for order alongside tradition, the greater part of the theoretical debates on the European continent since then have been characterized by the attempt to reestablish, at least in part by artificial creations, the stability taken away in the Revolution. One can cite as examples German doctrines on the state, such as Hegel's philosophy of law or the great works of Max Weber.

What is the practical problem lying behind these debates?

Most people do not read in books how they should act; they do not consult legal texts as to how they should behave and, as a rule, do not reflect very much when there are things to be done or left undone. Most ways of behavior and acting are determined by awareness that others in the past have acted likewise in similar situations and that others are acting in the same way now, that "one" behaves so or so. Habit, tradition, and handed-down custom—not deliberation, calculation, and reflection—determine people's everyday conduct. Whoever wants to change things must justify the change. The precept that all previous methods, ways of proceeding, governmental relations, and so on are the result of insights and explanations of previous generations and that they were not all fools is not known to everyone, but nearly everyone behaves accordingly. It is also so in politics.

Revolution interrupts this process of acting according to traditional practice, and step by step imposes changes. It creates situations in which much is no longer self-evident, by the invasion of violence, by new maxims, and the rise of new ruling groups. The continuity of events is interrupted. And the interruptions make people aware of the variability and fragility of their social and political relations. *One can send rulers and ruling groups to the devil.* The revolution, which brings forth a new government and a new political order, is a different, tangible instructor, which cannot be misunderstood. *One can send rulers and ruling groups to the devil.* This holds true also particularly for postrevolutionary governments, which came to power through revolution and obviously cannot declare it illegitimate without disputing the basis of their own rule.

The loss of tradition, wellspring of stability and authority, compels the new rulers to seek a new source of authority. And if they do not succeed, as in America, in creating a new constitution accepted by all, further revolutions and violence are inevitable consequences of the first overthrow.

After the first manifest breach in historical continuity and tradition, the more cogent question is why no further revolutions occur, rather than the question as to the reasons for later subversions. This question, like the question as to the conditions made the French Revolution possible, stands at the center of Tocqueville's reflections on this matter. And his researches produce a number of interesting results. But it would not be correct, in my opinion, to interpret them as "contributions" to a general theory of revolutions.[166] First, this would not correspond at all with Tocqueville's aim, and secondly, it seems to me that this concept of general theories is an extremely dubious enterprise, for "what it grants to the human mind in breadth, it takes away in precision,"[167] and the latter is Tocqueville's concern.

Tocqueville's works and investigations into the French Revolution are characterized by the attempt to present the discontinuities and continuities of French history, and to make distinct in their historical development the problems of France that had become obvious following the several overthrows. They are, like almost all great works on the French Revolution, an attempt to determine the state of society, and thus a contribution to forming a new understanding of itself by the new France.

Conditions shaping the revolution

One of the most important preconditions favoring the development toward revolution in France was the widening, gaping disparity between the wealth and education of the upper bourgeoisie, on the one hand, and, on the other hand, the lack of moral influence of the Church hierarchy and the impotence and humiliation, in actual fact, of the nobility.[168] Nobility and Church hierarchy had long ago been shorn of their political responsibilities and the functions of their class (settling local affairs, care for the population, and so on), and were using their unjustified privileged status only for economic advantage.[169] Political leadership, responsibility, and the function of maintaining order of the so-called political class had been lost long ago; their privileges had been reduced to commercial and economic prerogatives (tax privileges, for example) which no longer corresponded with any political function. The citizen's hatred for these prerogatives for which no one could see any basis was therefore all the greater.[170]

Comparing France and England, Tocqueville states further that one of the important preconditions of the Revolution in France was an intellectual climate that nurtured revolution.[171] The rise of a class of intellectuals—Tocqueville calls them writers (*écrivains*)—who were devoid of all practical political experience, owing to centralization of power and their special situation in society, became one of the decisive conditions for the French Revolution, of decisive importance not only for the eruption of violent events, but for the course of the Revolution.[172] The public debate conducted and decided by these intellectuals was determined by the discussion of general ideas and concepts, of doctrines and political dogmas, which lacked a close connection with the concrete problems of society. This debate directed to general and abstract doctrines led to a lack of reasonable reform ideas, which could have been carried out without revolution.[173]

A search for a new solution, which also caught up the rulers, took place at a time characterized by the inability of the ruling class to recognize the problems or extent of the crisis, or to develop reasonable reform ideas themselves. The rulers were not only isolated from society and no longer represented it at all; they were unable even to realize this fact. The practical intelligence traditionally instilled in the rulers failed both to analyze the state of consciousness of society and to devise reforms suitable for the new situation.[174] The debate over constitutional principles, abstract, formal justice, and designs for an order drawn from philosophical systems lay beyond the horizon of the political rulers. The rulers took no notice at all of what was actually happening in society, nor of what threatened them, because they failed to recognize the "debate of dreamers" as a menace to the political order.

Tocqueville emphasized that investigation of abstract doctrines is more important than the practical thoughts of the rulers for analysis of the prerevolutionary situation in France, and in this connection he terms the debaters of abstract principles of the Enlightenment "dreamers."[175]

His criticism is directed at those convictions of the Enlightenment that one could design and establish any given social order from a desk, and so reach both human and absolute justice without God. He directed his criticism also against the fact that the debate in French society over principles and doctrines did not deal with concrete problems of French society, had no real locus to which it was related, and had no social and political reality by which it could be explained.

The dreamer and ideologist who flees the world with his fantasies and "models" does not move in the world of tangible experience, which is for the awake and alert the sure area they experience in common, and the locus of ordered thinking, speech, and action by man. Probably one of the causes of the radical dynamics of ideological revolutions lies in the separation of the literati from reality, a separation that shaped the ideas of the revolutionaries. Tocqueville emphasizes this fact for the French Revolution and criticizes the divorce of the writers of the Enlightenment from the realities of their country.

And in fact revolutionaries naturally must necessarily lose their footing if they do not think and act in observance of concrete conditions and facts in any given society. The development of abstract system "models" divorced from concrete facts and the belief that everything is available to the initiator, denotes an unworldliness in the minds of the revolutionaries, which together with the possibilities of action in the revolution inevitably leads to fantastic results. Thus the locus of the Revolution became in fact primarily the minds of the revolutionaries; society, its institutions, and finally the citizens were disposable objects to be arranged as the mind of the revolutionary pleased.

Unworldliness (*Weltlosigkeit*) and general ideas regarding mankind consequently led the revolutionaries to a great passion for the new order, which took no account of the reality they found. The world was to be shaped according to their dreams, and the Revolution took the direction of concepts of the revolutionaries ever more remote from reality. The thinking of the revolutionaries, increasingly intoxicated by their own radicalism, is understandable. No longer freedom but the Revolution itself and its continuation against bristling opposition of social reality became the goal of their plans.

Tocqueville looked upon this tendency to perpetuate the Revolution as being primarily based on the fact that the "true goal of the Revolution was not so much a form of government, but a social order, not so much the seizure of political rights, as the destruction of privileges."[176] This signified that the Revolution's goal was social equality and would continue so long as the last great privilege, property, remained.[177] Tocqueville did not pursue these thoughts on interpretation of the French Revolution to their ultimate conclusion of complete social equality,[178] but states that the newly risen "race" of revolutionaries was opposed so violently and tempestuously to the rights of individuals, because they came from an unknown breed "turbulent and destructive."[179]

The intellectual leaders of the Revolution attracted a following in 1789 that was not drawn to the later dominant desire for stability and peace. At the time of the outbreak of the Revolution, France was not industrialized and had no population "needing inner peace and believing it was absolutely necessary for living."[180] Here Tocqueville set forth a thesis lately espoused by Herbert Marcuse, who, of course, starts from an entirely different frame of reference, and combines it with the imputation that with the nonoccurrence of the "last" revolution the kingdom of freedom has been missed. Marcuse tells us indeed that a revolution would be impossible today because of the manipulation of consumers' desires and their disciplining in the industrial work process, as well as because of the increased conveniences offered by industrial corporations. Tocqueville speaks likewise (but without the overtones of Marcuse, who expects deliverance through revolution) of "the many small conveniences which become necessities of the nations of our day, and make inner peace essential for them at any price."[181]

Tocqueville knew very well that there are economic conditions that favor the outbreak of a revolution;[182] but for him the set of mind of the revolutionaries, of the masses following them, and of the rulers attacked by the revolutionaries was of decisive importance, not only for the outbreak, but also for the course of the revolution.

The course of the revolution

In the year 1789 the whole French nation was seized by a revolutionary and political spirit, which lifted everyone above his narrow personal economic, social, or class interests. The common welfare determined the actions and thoughts of the actors: "I do not believe that in all known history anywhere in the world there was a comparable number of people who were so earnestly guided by the public weal, who so sincerely forgot their own selfish interests, were so completely engaged in the contemplation of a great work, were so ready to risk everything most dear in life to men, and were so exalted in their hearts to rise above small passions. This is the common cause of the passions, the courage, and the devotion from which proceeded all the great deeds which the French Revolution was to accomplish."[183] In these words Tocqueville depicts the intellectual climate immediately before the outbreak of the Revolution, and it must not be overlooked that in this enthusiastic description there is also discernible a critical aloofness to the *juste milieu* of his time and to the shopkeeper spirit politics apparent in the later revolutionary development Tocqueville experienced.

How was this spirit of a new beginning, of freedom and selflessness, lost? How was it possible that the French from 1789 to 1799 gave up their love of freedom so completely and forgot the value of freedom?

The overestimation of real possibilities, which led to the desire to reform each and every thing, which did not restrain itself, but wanted to alter old customs, viewpoints, and settled habits, in fact everything in society all at once, and which led to a general disruption of the moral world, finally forced the collapse of the revolutionary spirit. The dream of revolutionaries cannot last forever. The knowledge of the revolutionaries strays too far from the concrete facts of society. The pressure of actuality forces them back to reality. Experience, which deductive reasoning cannot rearrange according to its conceptions, destroys the dream world of utopian speculation. In this connection, Tocqueville speaks of a fall (*chute*) which brought revolutionaries back to earth.[184] This fall, namely the invasion of reality into the dreams and literary phantasms of the revolutionaries, leads to that peculiar breach in the revolutionary conviction, which is probably the chief characteristic of the course of the French Revolution.

The revolutionary rouses from his dream, awakened by the hard defeats experienced with a resisting society, and is thrown back on himself and his personal interests. The result is, that if he cannot achieve the total freedom he dreamed of, he tries to save the fruits of the Revolution at least for himself. A new selfishness spreads far and wide after hopes are shattered. "What demoralizes people most in long revolutions is not so much their errors, or even the crimes they commit in the fire of their passions and faith; rather, it is the contempt they sometimes feel afterwards for that faith and those passions which impelled them to action. Now they are exhausted, sobered, and disillusioned, and finally turn against themselves and conclude that they have been childish in their hopes, ridiculous in their enthusiasm, and still more ridiculous in their devotion."[185]

Now everyone recollects his own selfish interest, which in

his enthusiasm he thought he could abandon. Now society and politics are regarded as means to pursue private socioeconomic goals.[186] Society has become only a stock corporation in the eyes of the citizens. And the Revolution? It is still approved. Not because it attempted to establish freedom; freedom was sought and not attained. The Revolution is approved as the creator of a new order that allows everyone to pursue his private material fortune. The Revolution is approved because it has brought about the abolition of the nobles' privileges, and everyone wants to reap the harvest—especially in the economic sphere. The society of consumer hedonists, of economic citizens, takes possession of the legacy of the Revolution, which missed its original goal, freedom.

The Revolution had abolished the old privileges, had destroyed traditions and the feudal order handed down as axiomatic, accepted fact. Its desertion from the pursuit of freedom and self-government had opened the way to the pursuit of property and private individualism, and became its determining factor. This personalistic attitude of citizens and rulers, as well as the ever-present virulent utopian goals themselves, now proved to be menacing for the new order; instead of the pursuit of freedom, craving for security, protection against utopian dreams, and stability came to the fore, since these alone made the pursuit of economic goals possible. Tranquillity and stability were no longer basic conditions for freedom, but the highest goal itself in the political order.[187] The political constitution was viewed as subordinate to this goal, and a potential usurper could easily foster the impression that he could better guarantee desirable stability than could the republic. In the eyes of the citizens interested in tranquillity, the successful *coup d'état* of Louis Napoleon shifted the burden of proof to those who opposed it; the goal of security had made freedom expendable.

So despotism became the heir of the Revolution, which, frustrated, replaced its goal of freedom with the pursuit of prosperity. An all-powerful bureaucracy guaranteed the desired stability to the country and wangled for itself the right to monopolize politics and exclude the citizen from general matters, which became the affair of the central government and its officials and servants.

The dynamics of the revolutionary process

At the start of the Revolution the social status of the nobility and the Church hierarchy, obvious in economic privilege, stood in contrast to the significance of the rising upper bourgeoisie. Social institutions were not suited to the new situation and the essential needs of people.[188] The lack of sense of reality and of practical experience on the part of the revolutionary intellectuals, who were the foremost representatives of the revolutionary spirit, created in the course of the Revolutionary process a new contrast between revolutionary goals and the actual fact and possibilities in society caused by their actions. The revolutionary process broke up on the reality of social opposition, which proved to be stronger. The Revolution changed its direction; no longer freedom, but the pursuit of equality determined its course, and the Revolution flowed into the dictatorships of Napoleon I and Napoleon III. Freedom was sacrificed to equality. This renunciation of freedom was the consequence of the disillusionment of the revolutionary movement, which forswore its own ideals and wishful dreams, and pursued in its place *petit bourgeois* dreams of material prosperity and the economic stability that made prosperity possible. But the dreams and illusions of the revolutionaries, strangers to practical common sense, penetrated the mental subculture of society, where they lived on and threatened to intervene again in politics with their radically egalitarian demands.[189]

In order for the wasted revolutionary impetus to become effective again, a segment of the politically leading class had to assume leadership. "The experiences of the past seventy years have proved that the people *all alone* cannot make a revolution. So long as this essential element of revolutions is dependent on itself, it is impotent. The people becomes irresistible only at the moment it is associated with a segment of the leading class, and the latter will provide moral support or material collaboration if it has nothing to fear from the people. This is the reason that in the last seventy years, whenever the government seemed strongest, the onset of that sickness occurred, which brought it low."[190] In other words, the cause of the alternation between stable phases and revolutionary events in the course of the Revolution lay in the spiritual dichotomy of French society, whose common outward order was not ensured by a corresponding community of spirit. As soon as the appearance of outward tranquillity gave a false image of continuing stability, the segmentation of society occurred. The revolutionaries of the leading class assumed they could ally themselves with the masses without danger to the outward order, and a new phase of upheaval began.

Tocqueville's dilemma

Tocqueville refers again and again to the great traditions of the French Revolution of 1789, but also declares that it had been unnecessary, that its goals could have been achieved without upheaval in a process of reform. He takes a similar attitude toward the Revolution of 1830. Again in 1848, Tocqueville was an aloof critical observer without a clear viewpoint, and as foreign minister he played a most unfortunate role in the suppression of the republican uprising in Rome.[191]

Thus, Tocqueville's attitude remained ambivalent; no matter how eagerly he greeted and accepted the republican results of revolutions from time to time, he likewise kept his distance from revolution itself. His goal of stabilizing order for the sake of freedom caused him to reject any new commotion in a France ground down in revolution. Hence, in 1848 he quickly took his place in the camp of the "friends of order," which formed a large association supporting stability in relations at almost any price. His ideas of step-by-step adaptation of the current order by reforms and gradual changes, which he admired in British reform policy,[192] made him applaud the fruits of revolutions, although he viewed the basic event most critically. That was the dilemma of Alexis de Tocqueville, the man in politics.

2
Alexis de Tocqueville: The Political Man

The attempt to make of Alexis de Tocqueville a "modern" social scientist is valid, if one ignores the fact that the main part of the life history of this man was devoted to active politics, and not to social science.

We have already shown that his great works on America, on the French Revolution, as well as his *Recollections,* were produced at times when he was forced by political conditions to withdraw from professional or political activity. Tocqueville was a political man, and one of the causes of the peculiar fascination of all his works is most certainly the perplexity in which he addresses and investigates the subjects of his works, and which influences his kind of analysis.

Tocqueville's works on America and the French Revolution are not contributions to any—however designed—general theory of sociological, politological, or historical design, but attempts at clarifying concrete conditions of society.

Tocqueville looks upon both American democracy and the French Revolution as social processes in which he participates. As a spiritual representative of postrevolutionary France he articulates his understanding of French conditions, and in his mind and his works his interpretation of the republic is clarified. And this clarification of his own specific experiences is also the purpose of his reflections and writings.

He never intended to write a general theory. On the contrary: "General ideas are no proof of the strength, but rather of the insufficiency of the human intellect; for there are in nature no beings exactly alike, no things precisely identical, no rules indiscriminately and alike applicable to several objects at once. The chief merit of general ideas is that they enable the human mind to pass a rapid judgment on a great many objects at once; but, on the other hand, the notions they convey are never other than incomplete, and they always cause the mind to lose as much in accuracy as it gains in comprehensiveness."[1]

The insight Tocqueville formulates here should cause analysts of social phenomena both to exercise great restraint in formulating "general laws" and, on the other hand, to keep constantly in mind the close relation between historiography and social science. The author of *Democracy in America* explicitly points out that the development of general concepts and the acceptance of universal laws is a crutch for human reason, which helps it in its weakness, but at the same time proves its weakness.[2] The universality of statements, laws, and concepts is based on the finite nature of human possibilities for experience; and to assert out of this need a general and universal explanation which one moreover believes, and contents himself with, would be imprudent and certainly no indication of excessive wisdom.

The more general a statement and the greater the claim to general validity of a statement concerning social phenomena, the less is the probability that any specific phenomenon is adequately described. In addition, systematic, closed, all-embracing abstract explanations and assertions of general laws must ignore the free person acting concretely, must consider him as only a cog in the running of a process that cannot be influenced. In his *Recollections*, Tocqueville suggests he knows the source of those general theories and their claim to explain everything: vanity and laziness. He states it more politely when he writes that authors discovered "these exalted theories . . . in order to appease their vanity and lighten their labors."[3] "For my part," he writes, "I hate these absolute systems, which make the whole course of history dependent on great, momentous basic causes all linked together by the chain of fate, and delete men more or less from the history of the human race. I find them narrow in their pretended grandeur and false in their appearance of mathematical truth."[4] Vanity which, according to Tocqueville,[5] is godfather of the production of general theories explaining mankind, should not be simply understood as the attitude of a man who promotes himself before his compatriots and wants to shine before them. In the term "vanity" there lurks also something of that "metaphysical revolt" of which Albert Camus speaks, when he describes the attempt of humans who, in modern times, wish to take the place of God.[6]

In fact, the above-cited passages from Tocqueville on the inadequacy of general concepts are connected with an explicit delimitation of human knowledge, its limitations and its obtuseness in contrast to the omniscience of God. Indeed, it seems not incorrect to me to regard the stupendous attempt at a general explanation of history or the development of a general law of human activity and the formation of human society as an undertaking in which man presumes to a divine position.

We humans find ourselves in the situation of a swimmer in a rough sea knowing nothing of shorelines, maps, or currents. Thus, only very modest statements can be made on the structure, development, or direction of social movements. Only misunderstanding of his own situation can mislead a social scientist to develop a program of universally valid social scientific law formulas and divinely raise himself out of the sea— at least in his own mind.[7]

Yet the alternative to the universal explanatory theory of human activity and human history certainly need not be a total restriction to describing phenomena and episodes directly under our noses. One must simply bear in mind that one enters the realm of the uncertain and the probable when speaking of general questions. Insight coupled with modesty are then the virtues of a social scientist, who is intelligent but also cautious in his propositions.

In order to acquire this attitude the social scientist must be ready (a) to judge his perceptions without bias, (b) to recognize the limitations of human perception, and (c) with this knowledge to renounce any claim to complete, universally comprehensive explanations. This wise renunciation will often not occur without a crisis in one's consciousness, soaring heavenward, which is brought back to earth by experience.

Tocqueville lived through such crises. In a letter to Charles Stoffels he wrote: "When I began to ponder, I believed that the world was full of demonstrated truths. But when I desired to proceed to observe subjects, I could perceive nothing but doubt which could not be untangled. I really cannot tell you, dear Charles, in what a horrible situation this discovery put me. That was the most unfortunate time of my life. . . . Well, finally I convinced myself that the search for an absolute demonstrable truth is likewise a search for the impossible, like the search for complete happiness. It is not so that there are not some truths which deserve the complete conviction of men; but rest assured that there are only a very few of them. For the infinite majority of subjects which we must necessarily become acquainted with, we have only probabilities and approximations. To despair of this is to despair of being a human."[8]

This clearly formulated insight into reality and the limitations of human perception, and the emphasis on the character of approximation and probability of most assertions about structure and development of the world, society, and humans, is easily recognized as the unavoidable reality of the *condicio humana*. But Tocqueville knew the desire and urge for final certainty only too well as the craving of his own psyche. He knew, though, that to yield to this urge of the psyche would be a dangerous concession to something that would divert him from concern for truth. An "intellectual sickness" was torturing him incessantly, he wrote in 1848 to Royer-Collard. "It is an unbridled and irrational passion for certainty." Experiences showed daily, he stressed, that the world can be comprehended only in probabilities and approximations, but still, he continued, "I feel in the depths of my soul the yearning for the sure and the complete growing indefinitely."[9]

This "appetite" for certainty and completeness (brother of the nagging doubt also driving him),[10] which he recognizes as the yearning of his mind and fights, is probably one of the causes of the irritation and nervousness that Alexis de Tocqueville reveals in letters to his closer friends, when he describes his difficulties in writing. He has to hold his mind in balance, and the effort not to fall into pseudocertainties makes writing a torture of the soul for him. His soul is always restless. Tocqueville seeks this unrest. In our studies of his struggle with questions of religion, we have shown that he believed he could find spiritual peace only in dogmatism, and he refused this for himself. He feared he would never emerge from this kind of peace.[11]

Therefore, he wanted to keep his spirit constantly in searching movement so that his soul would not petrify. This purpose was also served by his dedication to politics, which activity he sought as much as close friendship—all of which should prevent him from falling into a state of melancholy and unreality. "I compare a person in this world," he wrote to Kergorlay, "to a traveler pressing on constantly into an ever colder region, who has to exert himself more, the farther he proceeds. The great sickness of the soul is coldness. In order to combat this evil, one must not only maintain the living movement of his soul by labor, but also by relations with his equals and the affairs of the world."[12]

For Tocqueville, life in society with his equals had an existential quality, and his works not only testify to his inner dialogue with the world of men, they are a continuous attempt to discuss things with his fellow citizens.

Yet this does not mean that he gave himself up entirely to the world of politics and opinions. On the contrary, Tocqueville struggled to maintain an aloofness from the current climate of opinion. We know from a number of letters that, after he had made up his mind on a subject of his research, he strove to ignore available literature dealing with and describing the same theme.[13]

The author of *Democracy in America* stresses that with his book on America and his studies on the *ancien régime* and the French Revolution he took pains to use exclusively documents and interpretations of the participants. Although it is improbable that Tocqueville could screen himself off completely from current representations and interpretations, he succeeded in keeping himself from accepting prevailing opinions on the various subjects of his studies.

Anyone who has written about a problem area knows the difficulty caused by the fact that, as a rule, he is not the first to address the subject area. On the one hand, one is happy to find available material already critically analyzed; on the other hand, it is hard, with those analyses in mind, to free oneself of prevailing interpretative patterns and to study available materials and subject problems without prejudice from accepted judgments and prejudices. Even as, and especially as, an analyst of social phenomena, one remains a citizen of the society of which one writes or in which one must imagine oneself in order to write about it. The experiences one has in society relate not only to the supposed "hard facts," but also to the opinions and interpretations that prevail in society as in social science. So Tocqueville took pains to keep an aloofness from the web of opinions and firm convictions of the society and social class in which he lived. Strong distrust and explicit skepticism of the prejudices of a leading class, which he considered partly naive wishful dreamers and partly simply corrupt, caused him to exercise reserve. He maintained his distance from the prevailing social interpretations of reality, and in this aloofness went so far as to take pains to take no notice of authors who wrote on his subjects.

That this procedure, if extended to a general attitude, raises problems, is obvious. For most certainly the world did not wait for any analyst. However clever one is, there were clever persons before him. But that was not Tocqueville's problem; he had, of course, read the great classicists from Plato to Montesquieu, and had been influenced by them. What Tocqueville refused to study was the current contemporary literature of his time, apparently to avoid being influenced by its interpretations, even unwittingly. So Tocqueville's studies and expositions circulate between the desire for certainty, which he knows he cannot fulfill, a distinct aloofness from the prevailing interpretations of political order, and his own efforts to influence the opinions of his compatriots.

OPINIONS

Tocqueville is very much aware that prevailing opinions are an important and extremely significant component of social reality. They are a part of "the moral and spiritual condition of a nation," which he lumps together under the term *moeurs* (morals, customs),[14] of which the identity of a society is made up, "the feelings, the convictions, the ideas, the habits of the hearts and minds of people," of which society is composed.[15] This conviction of Tocqueville's had to carry far-reaching consequences for him, too. If the realm of ideas and opinions is such an essential and determining factor of social reality, it lays a special responsibility on anyone who speaks out in society. Whoever makes speeches or writes books influences the socially relevant realm of opinions. He does not speak out on social conditions as if society were an "object" unrelated to him, but he speaks as a citizen among citizens in society. Every important assertion, insofar as it is taken seriously by relevant groups or classes of society, becomes itself a part of the realm of opinions, ideas, and convictions that determine society. And just this applies to Tocqueville's works to a special degree.

Tocqueville seems to be aware of this fact. We have already pointed out that a great portion of his published works is characterized by the aim of influencing the opinions of his compatriots.[16] Tocqueville is always a political citizen, even when he writes.

As a political and writing citizen he is fully aware of his responsibility for the consequences of what he says. This awareness also determines his attitude toward other authors and opinions. Thus, Tocqueville criticizes certain "views" that try to explain the actions of people and the fate of whole nations by causes lying outside the decisions of people.[17] He is not content to show that these views are strong; instead he attacks them as "cowardly" and "narrow," that is, he posits a relation of these opinions to the vices engendered by these views.

His consciousness of the political responsibility of the writer, surely sharpened by his studies of the revolutionary theoreticians of the *ancien régime*, led to a very massive critical dispute with the works of Arthur de Gobineau—a dispute that is fully comprehensible from this viewpoint, especially as to the terms used in the critique. When the racist work *Essay on the Inequality of the Human Race* was published, Gobineau sent a copy to his patron Tocqueville, and asked for his reaction. The reaction was crystal-clear. He thought this doctrine "very probably false and most certainly pernicious." Racial doctrine had nothing in common with his views, wrote Tocqueville, and he proceeded to point out the practical consequences arising from these theories, which "end in a very great diminution, if not removal of human freedom." He warned that "you may be sure, if the crowd which always follows the well-trodden path in spiritual questions accepts your doctrine, they would very quickly carry it over from the race to the individual, and from social abilities to all sorts of abilities." Racial doctrine has a negative effect on mankind, discourages the hopeful, and presses people to agree that their own and their national destinies are immutable. From this doctrine grow all the evils of inequality, such as hate, violence, distrust of equals, tyranny, and vulgarity.[18]

Tocqueville's rejection and criticism of racial doctrine are not made from the practical standpoint that he wanted to prove the incorrectness of the claims by showing their effects. The tenets of the book are false,[19] and moreover, its publication is dangerous because it favors "the vices of our times, (baseness, indifference, lack of initiative)."[20] People's freedom and responsibility, for Tocqueville, are not the result of the working of hidden forces or an invisible hand, which intervenes, if, for example, one just gives free rein to the passions of self-interest and pursuit of wealth. On the contrary, an important prerequisite of freedom is that people should be conscious of their responsibility and love freedom. Opinions and convictions of the citizens that pervade actions and habits are the basis of a libertarian order. Therefore, Tocqueville's published works are characterized—aside from their analytical achievements—by the effort to convince his compatriots of the value of freedom and to win them to it. They are a great discourse, which praises freedom, points out the threats to it, and shows the way to its establishment, procurement, and maintenance.

DIGRESSION: THE TRADITION OF RHETORIC

The assertion that Tocqueville's works can be looked upon and interpreted as a "discourse" is meant to point out that Tocqueville should be viewed less in the tradition of the political philosophers or even as a co-founder of political sociology than in the tradition of political rhetoric. This classification is not intended to define a "pigeonhole" into which one can assign Tocqueville. Rather, it is intended to facilitate access to Tocqueville.

Since the tradition of political rhetoric has largely fallen into disgrace in modern times,[21] it seems necessary to point out several peculiarities and particularities of political rhetoric, to avoid misunderstandings.

The majority of citizens today are easily inclined immediately to attach negative values to the word "rhetoric." When people speak of a rhetorical question or when one speaks of simple rhetoric or when a rhetorical proof is discussed, one thinks at best of overblown figures of speech, but usually of lack of sincerity, of demagogy, deceit, and diabolical arts of seduction. Primarily, this is connected with the fact that the speaker indeed is trying to influence or change the opinions and convictions of his fellow citizens. That this is looked upon as a negative aim is largely conditioned by the modern, but unrepublican concept that puts all articles of faith, convictions, and opinions on politics on one level, and then declares them "private affairs," which one at best ascertains through the backdoor of sociopsychological empiricism (*auf den Hintertreppen sozial-psychologischer Empirie*), but does not try to influence.

But the precise aim of the speaker is to influence the opinions and convictions of his fellow citizens. And oratory with an instructive aim should enable a speaker to change the opinions and convictions of his audience.

The tradition of rhetoric as instruction had its beginnings in classical Greece. Ancient rhetoric attained its first flowering in Athens with Isocrates,[22] and in Rome with Cicero.[23] This tradition was renewed in the Renaissance by Petrarch, Salutati, Bruni, Machiavelli, and others,[24] and later on by men like Montesquieu, Burke, and Madison.

The list of names is incomplete. It must not, however, be confused under any circumstances with the list of authors who wrote textbooks on rhetoric. When I speak of rhetoric, more is meant than the ability to speak and present convincingly.

To explain my classification of authors it seems fitting to make clear the particular qualities of rhetoric by setting forth its differences from philosophy. Both philosophy and rhetoric are concepts of education. Both proceed from the insight that the peculiarity of man is his faculty for *logos*.[25] The two schools separate at once over the two different meanings of the term. While the educational process of philosophy strives for wisdom and knowledge of divine and secular things, that is, puts ability to perceive and human reason at the center of virtues, the educational goal of rhetoric is the training of a citizen versed in public affairs, who through his speaking knows how to "teach, converse, but especially move and convince" his fellow citizens.[26] In other words, an orator is a man of practical politics, who tries to be effective in the world of opinions and customs, in society with his equals. The orator seeks less for new insights into the reality of this world and human coexistence, less for most precise and sure knowledge, and more for influence on the opinions of the masses. The subject matter in the training of an orator is indeed acquaintance with constitutions and practical philosophy,[27] but his interest in these subjects is founded on his pursuit of power and influence, while the philosopher analyzes constitutions and practical questions in the light of his search for the best constitution and the "good life." While the orator sees the purpose of his life in the republic and in collaboration with his equals, the philosopher is concerned with the search for truth beyond society and perfection of his virtues that, at least in part, transcend society.

The strong emphasis that the rhetorical educational process lays on speaking and argumentation makes clear its close relation to debate by the free and equal, that is, to a republic. And in fact all the foregoing authors were supporters and defenders of republican constitutional forms, not because their esteemed art of convincing is possible in republics, but because free speech and free debate of equal citizens constitute that public arena which allows people to make real their most human peculiarity, to be a speaking being.

But a republic of the free and equal—and we know this problem since Plato adduced it in the debate on the most reasonable form of human coexistence—is shaped by the government of opinions rather than the search of the philosopher for truth. That is, government in a republic is based on opinions of the citizens. The orator appeals to these, tries to use them for his purposes, and must influence them, if he wants to exercise power in society.

Since, in fact, government in free societies is based on opinions, an interpretation of a republic restricted to this description of facts leaves undebated the problem of good and just government. We know the explanation of all great

theoreticians of this problem:[28] the orator must be a philosopher or have the virtues gained through philosophy.[29] If, however, philosophers despise eloquence, the problem arises that
intellectuals lack eloquence and able speakers lack true knowledge.[30]

Seemingly, this problem is therefore soluble. The consciousness of the orator who wishes to win over public opinion
must be characterized by the philosophical search for truth.
In actual fact, matters are not so simple. The orator's goal is
power and influence and not insight into the truths of human
existence. If he does not want to lose all possibility of influence, he must make sure that the citizens follow him, and in
the best case (that he is truly guided by the philosopher's
search for truth and therefore by the virtues of love, of truth,
justice, and reason) will utter no untruth, but often find himself "forced" to silence on a great deal of unpleasant truths.
If one examines more closely the actual practice of an orator-
politician, it becomes clear that even the "model" of decision
in the case indicated above is a very unrealistic one. The problem, but not the practice, is laid bare. The active politician,
the orator, develops in the course of his life and political practice habits, a particular way of life and manner of thinking,
which—he is no philosopher—are determined less by love of
truth and more by pursuit of power and influence. He can
easily tend to rationalize to himself "a few simple truths,"
which supplant the habitual search for truth, and so damage
his spiritual honesty. The problem is suppressed,[31] but it is
not actually solved. So there is a contradiction, probably
solved by only a few great politicians, between the training
process, with its resulting fixed habits of philosophy, and the
fixed habits of the active politicians directed toward the
world of people and politics.

If republics do not wish to decay, however, they cannot
dispense with a reasonable political guiding class that influences and educates the opinions, attitudes, and convictions of
citizens. This holds true especially in times of constitutional
change; the alternative is oppression, suppression of debate,

and indoctrination, that is, loss of freedom. Written and spoken communication are irreplaceable instruments of free republics to clarify their sense of identity and to provide citizens with the symbols developed for this clarification process.

The necessity of influential and educative communication requires a presentation in which the orator teaches, pleases, and moves to action as he intends.[32] His own goal is the latter, and he only succeeds if he wins the applause of the crowd.[33] Hence, the orator-politician must be concerned with the totality of the opinions and sentiments of his fellow citizens, and he must accept most of them, if he wants to bring about a change of opinion on one or two points.[34]

Tocqueville is fully conscious of precisely this problem. Right at the beginning of the second volume of *Democracy in America*, he points out the fact "that no society can flourish without similar doctrines" and declares that without such "common beliefs" there can be no common society.[35] Tocqueville is speaking less of religious articles of faith, discussed three chapters later, than of beliefs (*croyances*) in a broader sense of common parlance, and means what people commonly think is true and right.[36] Although the explanations Tocqueville gives thereafter regarding both the average citizen and the *philosophes* seemingly deal with problems of perception and the search for truth, in fact Tocqueville exactly portrays the problems of the political orator.

"If man were forced to demonstrate for himself all the truths of which he makes daily use, his task would never end. He would exhaust his strength in preparatory demonstrations without ever advancing beyond them. As, from the shortness of his life, he has not the time, nor, from the limits of his intelligence, the capacity to act in this way, he is reduced to take on trust a host of facts and opinions which he has not had either the time or the power to verify for himself, but which men of greater ability have found out, or which the crowd adopts."[37]

In fact, the orator has to take prevailing opinion or the well-known insights of recognized authorities as a starting point, if he wishes to woo people away from an aspect of their views or influence their opinions.

Tocqueville speaks of the necessity of common opinions from which people proceed. The peculiarity of these statements consists less in his reflection regarding the situation of the investigator than in the direct relation of these passages to actions. He writes, "for without ideas held in common there is no common action, and without common action there may still be men, but there is no social body,"[38] and later declares that everyone who thus necessarily molds his opinions by trust in another opinion makes "his mind a slave; but it is a wholesome servitude, which permits him to make good use of freedom."[39] The freedom of which Tocqueville speaks here—as almost always in his works—is the freedom to act, and the investigator who really wishes to discuss several problems did not, in Tocqueville's realm of thought, occur apart from the experiences of his own thinking. Tocqueville is also speaking of himself when he speaks of the "unrest which . . . keeps him from a deeper penetration into some truth," as long as he strives for certitude in all spheres.[40]

This signifies that Tocqueville's description of the situation of a person in society, who has to take into account the opinions and convictions of others—which is also the description of an author—is an interpretation of his own situation.

ALEXIS DE TOCQUEVILLE:
THE ORATOR-POLITICIAN

Any public literary activity and in particular his own work on democracy in America, Tocqueville considered as a way of influencing the opinions of his compatriots, as education in consciousness toward freedom in the republic. In his speech of 3 April 1852 before the *Académie des Sciences Morales et Politiques* he formulated this idea of a political responsibility of a publishing political scientist most explicitly. All thoughts spread abroad among the people were of great significance for the continuation of political development, even though not noticed by the rulers. The idea of convincing the citizens, of influencing and forming their opinions, in a word, the idea that the writer should make an impact on society, that in this sense he is a political orator, was so dominant in Tocqueville's mind, that in his manuscript text he termed the academy a regulator (*régulateur*) of science,[41] although the published text notes only a "forum of freedom."[42]

The academy was not a political party, but he ascribed to it a regulating task, since he valued so highly the opportunity to influence opinions. The writer's task in a democracy was "to raise the faculties of men, not to complete their prostration,"[43] and so it seems to me necessary and legitimate to view Tocqueville's manner of propounding from the standpoint that he wished to convince, persuade, and promote the republic and its freedom. Tocqueville operated as a political orator in the best sense of the word.

Alexis de Tocqueville was a political man. This statement indicates more than the fact that from 1839 he held a seat in the parliament of the July Monarchy and a cantonal office in Normandy, that he was a member of the Constituent Assembly of 1848, and that until the *coup d'état* of Napoleon III he held office as deputy, and for a time as foreign minister. Tocqueville was neither a dilettante politician who, while engaged in writing books, occupied himself with parliamentary activities, nor a careerist who pursued his private interest by means of politics; politics was indeed the central activity of a great part of his life and mainly determined his thinking and actions. It appears to me that this fact is thus of great significance, because any analysis of the literary works of Alexis de Tocqueville must bear this in mind, if it is not to present an interpretation foreign to the view the author had of himself.

We stressed how marked the educative and promotional (for a republic) the accents in *Democracy in America* became, and we presented Tocqueville's work on the French Revolution as an attempt to gain clarity about the situation in France with a therapeutic aim. Tocqueville was also a political man when he wrote. He was a political man who wanted to fix the republic in the minds of the citizens, while informing the citizens and seeking to win them to support the republic. It follows that a number of formulations in his works are to be interpreted as other than texts of an exclusively reflective analyst.

Tocqueville's manner of arguing aimed at convincing obviously appears in political handbills and also very distinctly in speeches in parliament or in written committee reports.

The figures of speech employed there also appear in his books. They are a part of his way of arguing that endeavors to make plausible to the reader a decision held to be correct, by showing the absence of alternatives or by making clear the evil consequences of alternatives.

Tocqueville, who wanted to obtain majorities in Parliament or his electoral district, did not argue with false facts; instead he aimed at the known or supposed attitudes of those he sought to win over, in order to stir them to the desired action.

The argumentative figures of speech he employs sometimes sound nearly opportunistic, for example, when he terms liberation of the slaves inevitable and therefore summons parliament to carry out the inevitable at least in orderly fashion,[44] or when he denotes greater fiscal justice as honorable and just, but also necessary and prudent.[45] Tocqueville bases on tactical considerations even the apparent dispassion of his committee report to parliament endorsing the abolition of slavery. He had, so he said, avoided passions to the point of dispassion. "I wished to be painfully just and moderate in this matter, which has, I think, been so passionately debated," he wrote to Royer-Collard and asked him to judge whether his report promoted the desired success, freeing of the slaves.[46]

Tocqueville emphasizes the inevitability of liberating the slaves and adduces this as an argument for achieving the desired result. An argument aiming at winning allies is hidden in the form of an analysis. What he considers desirable he terms inevitable and thus invites even opponents to decide to accomplish the inevitable in orderly fashion.

Campaign rhetoric

An example of this rhetorical style of argumentation appears in the draft of a political basic declaration of Tocqueville, which probably dates to the year 1841.[47] The document reads as follows: "I experienced the fall of the Restoration with grief; too many remembrances and interests bound me to it, that it could be otherwise (1). I saw it also as a guarantee not only of the stability of the state (2), but even more of the freedom of the nation (3), if only the resistance which the Restoration opposed to freedom (4) could have been over-come by the legal means which was in the hands of France; this seemed possible and easy to me (5). But when I saw the almost unanimous agreement with which the nation acclaimed the revolution of 1830 (6); when I saw that everything which was strong and exalted, supported and defended it (7), I quickly rallied to that side, and I never made a secret of my opinions and the reasons which impelled me to this attitude (9). These are my reasons: I think that, if the Restoration had had a chance, it could have succeeded only by two means; by help from abroad, which I want at no price, or by support from the nation, but even then I think it would be a misfor-tune, because its predecessors are so opposed, so inimical to the ideas of freedom and the urgent needs which the establish-ment of freedom had rendered necessary for France (11), that I cannot place any trust in the change of heart of the Res-toration (12)—or in the honesty of the promises they would make, to regain the throne (13). I even do not trust the possi-bilities they would have to keep their promises, once they were in power (14). I would foresee so much misery in our country with the return of the Restoration, so many sacrifices of the most varied sorts, that I would try to prevent them with all my strength (15). So I try, honorably and loyally, to consolidate the satus quo (16); but, at the same time I sup-port to the best of my ability the regular establishment of civic liberties (17), which no opposition can suppress, which no efforts can overcome (18). I put forward no reservations against the victory of civic liberties, except that of protecting them against their own license (19). These opinions, these ideas, which in my conscience I hold to be true and salutary, are the result of the study of events (20), they will be the settled rule of my life (21). I wished to make my standpoint clear to you, so that you will know me thoroughly. Make whatever use of it you judge right. I stand for France and freedom (22)."

The document shows the singleminded orientation of Tocqueville's political thinking and actions toward the goal of political freedom. As a corollary, the problems Tocqueville, tied by so many bonds to the Legitimists, had to contend with, became apparent. The Legitimists considered him a traitor to their cause, while citizens and Liberals suspected him of being a disguised Legitimist. He, however, kept his cool distance from groups and factions. The coolness of his attitude allows him to argue in a completely impartial way. At the end he writes: "These opinions and ideas . . . are the result of the study of events (23)."

By his basic attitude, he would have favored a libertarian constitutional rule of the French royal house. Both his family tradition and his private interests (1) and also the stability derived from such rule (2) make him think a constitutional monarchy to be desirable. The free rights of the people achieved by the Revolution could, he thinks, be easily wrested to the restored monarchy (3). The justification for the rule of the restored dynasty would lie in political freedoms, which, if they prevailed, would reconcile tradition and freedom in a stable order (4); in fact, however, Charles's opposition (5), was not overcome by legal reforms, but by revolution. By the Revolution of 1830, French history had taken another road, and since Tocqueville was concerned solely with the establishment and securing of political liberties, and not this or that ruler (4, 17, 18, 22), he had to make a decision. What at first appears to be an opportunistic change of mind, Tocqueville's admission that he quickly went over to the camp of the victors (8)—a change justified first of all and apparently primarily by the unanimous agreement and support for the revolution (6, 7)—is laid open for rational examination by the announcement of a public presentation of his reasons. The way in which Tocqueville reveals these reasons is an invitation to every friend of freedom, particularly every reasonable Legitimist not blinded by hatred, to follow Tocqueville's decision.

What were Tocqueville's motives? One possibility for restoration of the rule of King Charles X is by violent establishment with foreign aid; this way is rejected at once without giving further grounds (10). The enmity to freedom of an imposed rule is obvious and does not have to be argued.

Much more important are the considerations that the restored rule of the period before 1830 could be established anew by the will of the great majority of Frenchmen. This brings up the question whether any rule would not correspond with freedom, if established by national approval.

Would it not then be a justifiable endeavor for Tocqueville, as always a scion of an old Legitimist family, to fight for this form of return of the Bourbons? Even this solution appears impractical to him; indeed, he declares, a restoration of the old regime would be a misfortune.

First of all, the old dynasty has become untrustworthy. Its opposition, even enmity toward political liberties has discredited the royal line (11), and one can no longer trust the Legitimists when they now, hoping to restore the old royal power (13), claim they have had a change of heart (12). But aside from this lack of credibility, Tocqueville argues that all those who would hold political office in a new restoration, and would be charged with counseling the king and influencing his policies, are not friends of freedom. The king would be unable to keep his promises (14), even though he had good faith; no king can continually act against his closest counselors. Bloodshed, probably civil war, and many miseries for the country, as possible consequences of the return of the king, make Tocqueville an opponent of Legitimist hopes (15), as does his conviction that this return would not serve his central goal, freedom, by which he judges the quality of a political order.

The document was intended for the enfranchised citizens of his electoral district in Valognes. The Tocqueville family was well known and respected there.[48] He was regarded as a Legitimist in the family tradition and so used his prestige to win over adherents of the old regime to the new constitution. He makes known that a restoration would only bring misfortune to France—no matter from what motives one might think it desirable (15). While he indicates his own necessity to rally to the new constitution and invites the reader to carry out his candid considerations (22), he also wants to gain supporters for his desire for consolidation and stabilization (16). This is a thoroughly comprehensible and plausible line of argument. Tocqueville's sovereignty, which supports freedom and is not concerned with attachment to this or that group, took him into opposition to Legitimist hopes and endeavors. Yet the logical consequences of turning against the Legitimists do not lead to an unconditional approval of the existing situation. He truly wishes to exert himself for consolidation of shaky conditions, (16) but this desire for stability and order is no goal in itself. Order is a prerequisite, not the goal of freedom. He wants to support and promote the establishment of civic liberties with all his faculties (17, 18), and those liberties should have limits only at the point where they become arbitrary.

Tocqueville wishes to increase the number of friends of the constitution. His line of argument is obviously built on emphasizing the absence of any alternative to deciding for the constitution, at least for anyone who thinks orderly conditions necessary for the sake of freedom.

The apparently opportunistic cast of the first sentences of the draft reveals itself as political shrewdness in two directions. First, he can make plausible to his voters in Valognes his decision for the constitution by relating his earlier Legitimist attitude and his turning away from it—bearing in mind how his voters assess him. And secondly, he asks all those who originally were Legitimist in thinking, as he supposedly was, to consummate his reasons and his decision. The alternatives to approving the new constitution are civil war, chaos, or tyranny. Hence, approval of the constitution is presented as essential without alternatives. And who would want civil war or tyranny?

Providence

This kind of argumentation, which presents approval of republican conditions as essential by contrasting the alternative of despotism, is familiar not only to the reader of his explicitly political pronouncements. Tocqueville also uses it frequently in the second volume of *Democracy in America*.

Right in the introduction to *Democracy in America* there is an especially plausible example of this type of procedure. Tocqueville knows that his readers, the educated classes of France, are incurably divided and quarreling over the question whether the development toward democracy should be promoted, fought, or answered by a withdrawal from public life. His book is directed at them, and the author appeals to their sense of responsibility. He insists that too many are occupied with the maintenance of former conditions or the senseless attempt to restore them. His criticism is that the rulers have never made an effort to prepare democracy: "It arose despite them and without their knowledge. The most powerful, intelligent, and most moral classes of the nation did not try to take it in hand, and guide it. So democracy was abandoned to its wild passions; it grew up like those fatherless children who grow up uneducated in the streets of our cities and know society only through its vices and its misery. . . . When it weakened through its own frivolity, the lawmakers hit upon the unreasonable idea of destroying it, instead of trying to teach and improve it; instead of teaching it the art of government, they only thought of how to eliminate it from the government."[49]

But Tocqueville did not want to prolong the debate over whether one should promote or fight democracy, and so adduces his concept of the inevitability of development to democracy, which makes the whole debate seem obsolete. The step-by-step progress toward equality of conditions is a work of Providence. Whoever opposes it is acting against history, against all insight, yes, against God himself.[50] Such endeavors would be unsuccessful, at any rate. "Everywhere we have seen the various occurrences in the lives of nations work out to the advantage of democracy; all men have aided it by their efforts, both those who intentionally labored for its successes and those who had no thought of promoting it; those who fought for it and even those who declared themselves its enemies; all were driven pell-mell in the same course, and all labored to one end; some despite themselves and others unwittingly, all blind instruments in the hands of God. The gradual development of the principle of equality is, therefore, a providential fact."[51]

This formulation, reminiscent of Hegel's "cunning of reason," is speaking of the general direction of the historical process. Its purpose is not to move the reader to unconditional acceptance of his fate. Rather, acceptance of democracy would end a fruitless debate, and the energies that have gone into it could be sensibly applied to construction of the republic. The argument of the inevitability of historical progress, which Tocqueville puts forward to avoid false approaches to the problem, culminates in the symbol "Providence." The use of this concept, it seems to me, does not indicate that Tocqueville infers a specific theory of history. "Providence," as Tocqueville elsewhere states,[52] is a commonplace of his time, and the emphasis on Providence that cannot be held back by human hands was readily understandable in a time where revolution, *coups d'état*, and several collapses of constitutions had made everyone thoroughly conscious of the limits of his personal ability to act.

Tocqueville, though, who brings the inevitability of development into his argumentation, is confronted with a problem, since, on the other hand, he insists upon the freedom of man to determine his fate. This brings to the fore the task of bringing the freedom of acting man into agreement with the inevitability of the process that presses toward democratic society.

The inevitability of the democratic revolution

For analysts of European revolutions there is obviously the common experience of the inevitability, of the irresistibility of revolutionary events, which leads, in the radical formulations of Comte, Hegel, Marx, and later for example, Trotsky and many others, to the belief in an extensive determination of the fate of classes, societies, and whole civilizations. The perception of the inevitability and irresistibility is related first to the destruction of the old order, which, especially in the case of the French Revolution, is seen as irrevocably removed. The predemocratic orders, ruled by a small political class determined mostly by birth, instantly and irrevocably belong to the past in that the authority of the rulers is no longer able to uphold the old order. It reminds one of the parable of the emperor's new clothes: when once the call rang out that the emperor was naked, the point of no return was passed. Suddenly, the appeal of potential rulers to their birth is no longer an argument, from which fact it is undoubtedly true that the decay of the authority of the traditional political class must have already proceeded markedly long before the events.

A second, even more solid experienced perception of observers of revolutionary overthrows can be added. The intervention of larger masses of people in events and their appearance on the political stage, their collective action, which visibly becomes a law unto itself in the course of a revolution, must have paralyzing and depressing effects on any objective observer. The classic remedies of politics appear not to play a role any longer. Since there are no responsible and sovereign leaders with whom one can deal, there are no possibilities to persuade and convince structural elites. Moods, rumors, slogans spread by anonymous persons, and anxieties of the masses determine events in many areas. There is seemingly no single person by whom events can be guided. The great mass, its moods and opinions, sets the climate produced by actions and events. The single, sovereign mover, who acts freely, seems to have abdicated; he has been superseded by the exponents of fluctuating moods and opinions of the aroused masses.

Tocqueville knew well that the events and developments that led to 14 July 1789, and the ensuing revolutionary developments after that date, were a segment of history that would not allow a return to the prerevolutionary social and political conditions.[53] Now his task was nothing less than to rescue the responsibility of the acting man, and thereby to rescue human freedom to act.

The rescue of responsibility and freedom of action

The above-quoted words from the introduction to *Democracy in America* are complemented in the viewpoint of the second volume. In the final words of his book, Tocqueville refers to the freedom of people and nations, which consists for him in that people decide by their actions whether the inevitable progress toward equality of conditions will lead to a society of slavery and despotism or to a society of free citizens. "Nations of our days cannot cause internal conditions not to be equal," Tocqueville stresses and continues, "but it depends on themselves whether the principle of equality will lead them to servitude or freedom, to knowledge or barbarism, to prosperity or poverty."[54] That is, he divides human affairs into two realms. One of these areas lies outside the power of men. An inevitable development presses societies toward equality and democracy. This cannot be altered by actions. But the question, which concrete form this democracy will take, how the democratic society and its citizens will be constituted, belongs to the other realm, for which people have to answer. They can deal with this. This separation between irresistible historical development and the free realm of human activity allows Tocqueville to introduce ethics and responsibility into his interpretation of social reality, despite the seemingly irresistible process that impels it. The apparently deterministic argument of Providence has on closer examination an opposite effect to that expected. It delimits the realm of people's responsibility for their own destiny, outlines the realm of free decisions, and points out the citizen's responsibility, which one cannot avoid by debate over the question whether democracy is desirable. Tocqueville asks in admonition—evidently of those who thought the process of development toward democracy had ended with the Revolution of 1830 and one could now pursue his own private pursuit of wealth—whether one could imagine that "democracy, which had conquered feudalism and kings, would shrink back before the merchants (*bourgeois*) and the rich."[55] Democracy cannot be halted, and the debate over it is pointless. Now it is a question of guiding a society of equals and giving it a structure in which freedom remains possible, freedom that formerly only the aristocrats enjoyed.

Thus, the real subject for debate is how to establish the political constitution of democracy. Only when the citizens recognize this realm as their own sphere of action, if they accept the aforementioned progress toward equality and devote themselves completely to matters that can be influenced by their actions, will the practice of freedom be possible.

In the introduction to *Democracy in America*, Tocqueville sets aside the arguments of a debate he considers pointless; it is not a question of whether equality will come, but which kind of spiritual and political constitution will determine it. A great part of *The Old Regime* is devoted to demonstrating that equality would have won out even without the Revolution. To oppose it is hopeless.

Tocqueville is concerned with freedom in the republic; that shall be the focus of the debate, which must not be distorted by sham problems and in which his important helpers shall not be diverted by reactionary dreams. Tocqueville is seeking allies in his promotion of freedom in the republic.

Proselytizing for the republic

Tocqueville wishes to convince his readers of the advantages of a republic. This desire is one of the grounds for the ambiguity noted by many writers in several concepts Tocqueville employs. It is the result of his attempt to give several expressions a meaning deviating from that of everyday speech.[56] Tocqueville's proselytizing intent, his pedagogic concern with the reader's mind,[57] is striking in *Democracy in America*. Again and again, the author interrupts his line of thought to tell the reasons for his manner of dealing with the subject, or to set forth his problems in presenting it;[58] the desire to speak directly to the reader through the text is obvious. The entire book is not unlike a written oration, a fact indicative of Tocqueville's intent, though this manner of writing was more common in the nineteenth century than today.

Tocqueville addresses his compatriots to win them to freedom in democracy. He states this explicitly in a number of letters. In 1835, he writes to his friend Louis de Kergorlay that he had not gone to America with the firm intent to write a book, that the idea had first occurred to him there. "I said to myself that every person owes an accounting to society with his thoughts as well as his physical strength. If one sees his compatriots in danger, it is his duty to come to their assistance."[59] And in December 1836 he writes to his close friend even more explicitly about the aims of his book: "To show people, so far as possible, what one must do to avoid tyranny and degeneration while becoming democratic. That is, I think, the general idea by which one can comprehend my book, and which will appear on every page of it I now am writing. To labor in this sense is in my eyes a *holy* occupation, and for it one should spare neither his money, nor his time, nor his life."[60]

Tocqueville's research and description of democracy in America is a plea to his French compatriots, who are to be converted to an orderly republican democracy that trains citizens in practical freedom.

The inference in the introduction, when Tocqueville speaks of a stabler and quieter future that he hopes God is preparing for the European nations, and then discusses America, takes shape more and more in the body of the text. Tocqueville not only invites his readers to follow him intellectually in his analyses, he tries to proselytize for the democratic republic. The alternative to the republic is not restoration of the old regime or rule by the aristocracy, but a Caesarean tyrant. "When I consider the present condition of several European nations, a condition to which all the others tend, I am led to believe that they will soon be left with no other alternative than democratic liberty or the tyranny of the Caesars."[61] The alternative presented to the reader is obviously meant to win him over to democratic freedom. In his writing, Tocqueville is always thinking of the effect his text will have on the mind of the reader, and the work is directed to this effect. He wants to convert, to convince. He is in the best sense of the word pedagogic.

Yet the teaching of freedom is not so simple that it can be based primarily on instruction, as we have shown. Freedom, the constitution of freedom, whose essence lies in practical activity, is not "learnable" solely or primarily through theoretical teaching. Tocqueville is entirely aware of this. "True information is derived mainly from experience; and if the Americans had not been gradually accustomed to govern themselves, their book learning would not help them much at the present day."[62]

The practical knowledge of rights and freedoms that the institutions of the American republic provides its citizens, makes associations, communities, juries, the press, and the whole body of local politics something like public schools in freedom, which shape the citizens' habits, morals, and manner of acting.

It follows, that in France, too, all this cannot be learned by reading books. However, Tocqueville taught, esteemed, and praised the wholesome effects of a democratic republic on freedom. Whom was he addressing; whom would he reach? For whom did he write? "There are persons in France who look upon republican institutions only as a means of obtaining grandeur; they measure the immense space that separates their vices and misery from power and riches, and they aim to fill up this gulf with ruins . . . they fight for their own advantage. . . . It is not to these that I address myself. But there are others who look forward to a republican form of government as a tranquil and lasting state, towards which modern society is daily impelled by the ideas and manners of the time, and who sincerely desire to prepare man to be free."[63]

The second group in France was still too small, and Tocqueville wanted to increase it; and he sought good friends of democracy in the social *milieu* of the old leading class he knew so well. It was a mixed bag of skeptical Catholics, who regarded democracy as an institution hostile to faith, of conservatives who were afraid of riots in the streets, and of Legitimists, who dreamed of the return of the Bourbons. Throughout he was concerned with citizens of the educated classes of France to whom he wished to make clear that there was really no longer any means to remain free, but the democratic republic.[64]

Social origin, family tradition, and his youth bound Tocqueville to these groups. But the course of his life, for example, his marriage with a middle-class woman, and his oath of allegiance to the Constitution of 1830, which led to his social isolation in Versailles, had alienated him from the social class into which he had been born. Tocqueville invites them all to go through his own process of development that had led him to approve the democratic republic. He wanted them to follow him politically and to renounce the dream of a return to the monarchy of Henry IV or Louis XIV.[65]

The French democratic republic could be successful only if it succeeded in converting "the most powerful, most intelligent, and most moral class of the nation" to leadership in public life and not to abandon democracy to "its wild instincts."[66] Tocqueville wanted to win these classes as allies so that they would undertake a task similar to that accomplished by the much admired Founding Fathers with their Federalist party.[67]

That Tocqueville looked upon the American Founding Fathers as models for potential founders of the French republic and republican traditions, becomes very plain from the following. Although he knew that, in founding the United States of America, the Founding Fathers faced an already existing decentralized constitutional order, local republics, and local freedom, which had already been decided,[68] he interpreted the American reality of local partial autonomy of federal states and communities as the result of a conscious decision of the Founding Fathers. They did not suppose "that a general representation of the whole nation would suffice to ward off a disorder at once so natural to the frame of democratic society and so fatal; they also thought that it would be well to infuse political life into each portion of the territory in order to multiply to an infinite extent opportunities of acting in concert for all the members of the community and to make them constantly feel their mutual dependence."[69]

This distortion of historical reality makes sense if one relates it to the very different conditions existing in France. The "decision" attributed to the American Founding Fathers is absolutely essential for France. What was provided to Americans by historical circumstances could be introduced in France only as the result of conscious deliberation. The supposed motives of Americans turn out to be arguments for a similar decision in France.

THE DEPUTY

Miserable conditions

Tocqueville is no armchair intellectual. For him, the politically active citizen, the publication of *Democracy in America*, is not simply the result of thorough observation and analysis of American society and its constitution. We have already shown the close relationship of this work to French reality. The publication of this book was itself a political act; not only because its great success brought Tocqueville nearer to his goal of a seat in parliament,[70] but also because the book constituted a momentous attempt to redirect the French Republic and its citizens spiritually, intellectually, and institutionally toward the good of freedom.

Alexis de Tocqueville, the spiritual representative of the French search for insight into the bases of postrevolutionary order, was also institutionally a political representative of France in the parliament of the French bourgeois monarchy from 1839 on.

If we now turn in our analysis to Alexis de Tocqueville the practical politician, it is not with the concealed intent (*Hintergedanken*) to squeeze him into the cliché categories of modern social science, or to investigate whether he put his "theories" into "practice" and where problems occur from this.

The subject of the following analysis is rather the dispute of Alexis de Tocqueville the deputy with the phenomenon of disorder in France.

In this regard Tocqueville's situation caused him mental distress. His political knowledge, his insights into the significance of opinions, articles of faith, and ideas for political order kept him from the modern false notion that any problem is soluble through laws or government actions, provisions of constitutions, or decrees. He knew that the locus of disorder is in the consciousness of the citizens and their representatives, and that unstable relationships are only a symptom. "Disorder lies not in the facts, it has penetrated deep into the consciousness," he declared in a parliamentary debate[71] and insisted that France's problem, which had to be cured, lay in the decay of public morals and political consciousness, and not in this or that measure of the government.[72]

But parliament was primarily concerned with governmental measures and projected laws, and the public consciousness was not at its disposal. It was occupied with the art of governing, with practical politics, which had to do with everyday needs and problems. Tocqueville knew very well how to distinguish this area of governing from political science, which was based on "the nature of man, his abilities, his needs . . . his passions."[73] But he also was thoroughly cognizant that the climate of public opinion, the opinions and notions of citizens on politics, is decisively influenced by government policy and the way in which parliament debated government policy.

Thus, the deputy from Valognes was forced to express his criticism and warnings concerning specific bills and debates on governmental declarations, in order to press from these to more fundamental problems. Tocqueville's parliamentary speeches set forth his criticism of individualism in direct relation to France and the policies of the country's governments. The constitutional proposals of Tocqueville as deputy of the nation made concrete his criticism of centralism, and his conviction as to the wholesome effect of local politics and his criticism of government policy as a whole make crystal clear how keenly he was aware of the fragility of the free national constitution.

These flowing thoughts from among Tocqueville's concepts of order are significant for our analysis. For this reason, we pay less attention to the loose alliances of Tocqueville in parliament, to his attempt to form an independent group of deputies, or to his defection from the ranks of the opposition on the question of the "Spanish marriage." What concerns us more are his attacks on individualism, administrative despotism, and the destruction of political consciousness by the government, which complement his criticism of the condition of French political society developed in *Democracy in America*.

As a deputy, Tocqueville considered himself as part of the opposition to the Guizot government. With one exception he voted with the opposition. But one must not overlook the fact that he also held himself aloof from his colleagues in the opposition. Tocqueville was anything but an accommodating deputy intent on systematically furthering his career. The same spiritual and moral principles that had made him world-famous guaranteed him attention and influence in the Chamber of Deputies but, since they in fact motivated him, proved to be an obstacle for the eagerly awaited great political career of the deputy from Valognes.

Even the defeat in his first candidature in 1837 was the result of his refusal to accept support as a candidate of the government. The government coupled its offer to help him in the campaign with expectations that he would help the government in parliament. But it was precisely this restriction of his independence that he wanted to avoid. He conducted his campaign without help from the government and barely lost.

Two years later he was elected. He already knew before his entry into parliament the state of the national representation, and even so was dismayed with the spiritual condition of the Chamber. This dismay was to remain with him all through his political life.

Through his election Tocqueville became a member of a parliament, whose transactions were diametrically opposed to his concepts of national representation in the service of freedom. The new political class, which had become the dominant class in France by the Revolution of 1830, was not like the revolutionaries of 1789. It was subject to unrealistic dreams of liberated humanity; but the "practical reason" that the leaders of the *juste milieu* took as the principle of their policy and thereby became the maxim of the whole country, was miserably petty. The typical deputy's principal aims were his own career, assuring reelection with government support, and exploiting connections for relatives, acquaintances, or influential citizens in his constituency.

There were no great controversies, and "the lack of great debates and clashes make a parliamentarian class of the deputies, who work for their own concerns, and to display their worth to the voters." The voting behavior of a deputy *vis-à-vis* the government depended on the granting or withholding of requests and demands for committee positions, offices, and honors by cabinet members. The parliament was largely depoliticized.[74]

It was more a socioeconomic clearinghouse than the central political institution of the country, and the deputies were more concerned with official positions, government contracts, or commercial privileges for constituents than with the fate of France. The transactions of the parliament were determined by the economic interests and career ambitions of the upper bourgeoisie.

The franchise according to the census (*Zensus-Wahlrecht*) that denied the franchise and the right of candidacy to the majority of the people made of the rich politically privileged persons who were misusing political privileges for their economic advantage. The new small class, defined by its economic position, was carrying out its pursuit of wealth by means of politics and thus was privatizing public life. The deputies were not representing the people, but their own selfish interests and careers, and protected against the free franchise they could do so unhindered. The direct result was a division between the people, shut off from politics, and their representatives. And so, Tocqueville concluded, the people got the notion "that political life was nothing but a game of personal careers . . . a game without reality." This was, he wrote to Beaumont, the main reason for the growing indifference into which the country was slipping.[75]

The politics of the deputies, concerned primarily with their private businesses and those of the upper bourgeoisie, produced no resonance in the people. The problems of order in French society, which perturbed Tocqueville, did not appear on the agenda. It was no wonder that after the very first session he told his fatherly friend Royer-Collard he could not be condemned simply to vegetate in parliament.[76] He felt the lack of great political debates and clashes that could lead to the formation of political groupings around the opinions expressed in debates, which in this way would draw into politics even those citizens who were excluded from the active and passive franchise.

The government was taking the easier path for it, but the more dangerous one for France. It held its majority in parliament together, not by propagating common ideas and opinions on policy, but by personal and particular advantages that it bestowed on the deputies. In this way, the debates became meaningless shadow-boxing, which no one could take seriously, and particularly which never reached the citizens outside parliament and drew them into the clash of opinions. The parliamentarians remained apart, among themselves.

The small scale of the disputes, the meaningless struggles, intrigues, and jealousies of the deputies and political leaders, repelled him. Tocqueville was indeed in parliament and took part in parliamentary work, but he equally kept his distance in the behavior of a critical observer with which he met events and persons. He was waiting for better times, which would correspond to his urge for political effectiveness in large issues, and condemned the state of general lassitude, which afforded him no room for action.

In two of his letters written in October 1841, he described both the insignificance of parliamentary reality and his tactic of waiting. He wrote to Ampère that even evil passions still displayed force, and that still seemed preferable to the atmosphere of general weakness surrounding him.[77] And to his friend Beaumont, likewise elected to parliament, and who was tending toward closer cooperation with Thiers, the leader of the opposition, he explained his reserved behavior: one must take a position on all important questions before the Chamber, but never bind himself too closely to any of the parliamentary parties. Any connection of that sort would bring more loss than gain. Even founding a new party offered no prospect of success. All one could do was to act as if alone, wait for favorable conditions, and remain available.[78]

Tocqueville's desire for fundamental disputes sharpened his perception of the miserable depth of the political situation and surely contributed appreciably to the aloofness and coolness that impress the readers of *Recollections* and those who study his correspondence and the writings he left.[79]

Here speaks a man who is in the midst of affairs, but keeps himself outside of them. And actually Tocqueville remained in partial self-chosen isolation during almost his whole time in

Parliament. He knew this and spoke of an "honorable, but sterile role," which stood in contrast to his desire to help determine the destiny of France through influence on politics, formatively and powerfully.

The rejection and aloofness Tocqueville displayed toward parliamentary business and naturally to parliamentary colleagues, too, did not remain hidden from them. True, he was admired for his perspicacity, his intellectual brilliance, and his reputation, but the respect of his colleagues was dampened by his aloof attitude, which was not such as to make him a great parliamentary leader. And his poorly developed rhetorical ability did not help to overcome this fact.

It is, however, an overly hasty judgment, seemingly characterized by categories of success and career, when J. P. Mayer writes that Tocqueville "failed as a politician . . . , because he lacked the hardness and unconcern of a political leader. . . ."[80] Already before 1848 Tocqueville, as politician, was actually one of the most influential deputies in parliament—in those questions he himself considered important enough to devote all his attention to.

"In fact," André Jardin writes mildly critically of similar statements of Beaumont, "Tocqueville's political career was anything but mediocre; under the July Monarchy he was the *rapporteur* of the Chamber on draft bills for abolition of slavery and prison reform, two of the greatest moral problems facing liberal consciences at that time. Likewise he was *rapporteur* of the Algeria Statute, a subject of passionate controversies. Toward the end of the regime he enjoyed a kind of moral authority, which, certainly never disputed, was strengthened more and more with the passage of years." This authority explains Tocqueville's important role in the Republic of 1848, in which he held a significant position on two constitutional committees and as foreign minister.[81]

Tocqueville's authority, called "moral" by Jardin, was based first and foremost on the fact that Tocqueville, unlike most of his parliamentary colleagues, was guided in his speeches and actions by a care for the maintenance of free relationships, and that he based his criticism of the government on very fundamental arguments.

Corruption of society by the government

"What has the government been doing for four years? . . . It replaces principles with private interests. It wins over every single person. How? By having regard to their opinions? No; by offering them favors, offices, and appointments. . . . Every day it suffocates political life, suffocates the formation of opinions and the continuance of memories. . . ."[82] With these words Tocqueville stated in 1845 his criticism of the Guizot government, which maintained itself in office by satisfying the private interests of the deputies supporting it. Petty interests, not common ideas and opinions, held the government majority together; no common concepts on a policy for France bound government, parliamentary majority, and voters supporting them; the cement holding together the governing group around and under Guizot was instead the obtaining and exploitation of personal advantages drawn from government power. "They influenced the voters by favors they gave them, and tried to influence the deputies by giving them the opportunity to distribute favors."[83]

This peculiar cartel of private interests made politics a self-interest enterprise of the government majority. And that had fatal consequences for the spiritual and moral state of the whole nation. So long as the government addressed the people in terms of their private interests and was not concerned with their opinions, convictions, and ideas, parliamentary alliances and changing coalitions of groups of deputies would remain a murky legerdemain of politicians without recognizable sense for the nation.[84] On the one hand, the politics of distributing favors trained the citizens to servility,[85] and collaborators profited. On the other hand, the citizens looked upon public affairs as something that they did not comprehend and that did not concern them. As a result, the country was sinking into indifference and apathy.[86] Yet political abstinence and retreat by the citizens into private life would lead to destruction of public morals, if deputies made their public offices almost as a matter of course instruments of their private interests. "I permit myself . . . to ask the majority whether to their knowledge in the last five, ten, or fifteen years the majority of those who vote for them out of personal or particular interests has not grown without ceasing; whether the number of those who vote for them because of (common) political opinions has not constantly diminished? I challenge the majority to declare to me whether around them and right under their eyes, a peculiar growth of these ways of behaving has not consolidated itself step by step in public opinion; whether base and mean morals are not being introduced, according to which a man who possesses political rights owes to himself, his children, his wife, his relatives the personal exploitation of these rights in their own private interest, whether this does not gradually lead to its becoming a sort of duty of a family father?"[87]

But the saturation of society and politics with the spirit of personal interest destroys political morals and threatens all society. "Has there ever been a great society in the whole universe without good morals, and was there ever a free society without them? . . . Any government which sows vice will sooner or later reap revolutions. . . ."[88]

Tocqueville insisted that he was not speaking as a moralist, but rather of questions of political order; but the decline of private morals was a consequence of the corruption of public morals,[89] and both threatened the stability of France.

What Tocqueville observed and criticized was the individualization of French politics. Each individual deputy was thinking of his own advantage, of advantages for his family and friends, and of privileges for his constituency. The deputy from Valognes missed the devotion to goals and passions for the whole country; he felt the lack of political motives beyond private self-interest (*sentiments désintéressés*) that would lead the nation, instead of dividing it. If the deputies no longer represented opinions and convictions, but only interests, "we will soon arrive at the extreme situation that we no longer represent ideas or people, but private interests, canals, and railroads."[90] And because the nation is not united by goals and desires beyond private interests, it does not look upon the existing order as a community. This again endangers the existing order.

Again in January 1848 Tocqueville gave warning of the consequences that the officially promoted and furthered individualism would have for domestic order. The consequences would be not so much a disruption of the outward order, but rather that the way of thinking and the consciousness of the French would slide into a condition of complete disorder. This was due primarily to the fact that the citizens not belonging to the class of the enfranchised did not even see their opinions represented in parliament. They therefore indulged in private dreams. One could not, declared Tocqueville, sneak past these problems and say that there was no revolutionary movement, and therefore there was no serious danger. "Look closely at what is happening in the working classes which, I admit, are quiet. It is true that they are not motivated by political passions in the narrow sense, as was the case before; but do you not see that their political passions have become more social? . . . Do you not hear that they constantly repeat that everything above them is inept and unworthy to govern them; that the distribution of goods existing till now in the world, is unjust; that property rests on foundations which are foundations of injustice? And do you not believe that when such opinions take root, if they spread in an almost general way, if they penetrate deep in the masses, that sooner or later, I know not when, I know not how, that they will sooner or later produce very formidable revolutions? . . . I think we are sleeping at present on a volcano."[91]

This volcano erupted in one month. Although Tocqueville himself emphasized that his admonitions were motivated less from a presentiment of impending revolution than the desire to shake up the parliamentarians,[92] he correctly recognized the unstable condition of society through the apparent calm.

Participation of the citizens

The political emptiness of the debates during the July Monarchy, the seduction to which the government was exposed in employing the powers of the central authority to bind citizens to it by offices and economic advantages, and the danger that the obvious depoliticization could become the entry gate for utopian dreams were the three great themes that stirred Tocqueville. They determined his deliberations on the constitution, his constitutional proposals after the Revolution of 1848, his criticisms of the government, and his fundamental reflections on French internal politics before the Revolution of 1848.

On the one hand, Tocqueville considered stable political relations indispensable for the success of the republic. The French had to become used to the fact that constitutions must not be changed with every passing fancy. On the other hand, the political and economic rights of participation of the people had to be gradually broadened, for only a constitutional, social, and economic order that more and more drew in all citizens would make the desirable degree of stability compatible with political freedom, and that was the objective.

In October 1847, Tocqueville drew up a manifesto at the instance of some friends, which was intended to make plain the standpoint of a group of independent deputies who were thinking of founding a party. This document, *On the Middle Class and the People*,[93] which although not published in his lifetime but which Tocqueville specifically cites in his *Recollections* and claims as his own,[94] is designed precisely to harmonize freedom and stability.

The manifesto begins with the declaration that a political movement was appearing in the people that had no echo in public institutions.[95] The parliament was not taking its task seriously. Since it was only an institution of the well-to-do bourgeois class, which was very homogeneous, there were no great political parties which could carry their controversies to the people. That was the cause of "this lassitude displayed by public life." The nation "was dozing off while listening, or was busy with its own thoughts."[96] That hoary phenomenon of French disorder, political dreamers who were not brought back to the earth of facts by experience and prudence, was present also in the July Monarchy.

SOCIALISM

But because the agitation among the people was now directed against the last remaining privilege, property, a new political battle-line would soon appear "between those who possess and those who do not possess. . . . The battlefield would be property; and the basic questions of politics would turn on more or less radical alterations in the rights of property owners.[97]

The current socialistic theories, which Tocqueville rejected, but with less intensity in dealing with them, owing to a certain incongruity,[98] had to be taken seriously because they were a sign of a dangerous tendency. A policy to overcome this situation had to pursue two aims in its legislation: "1. To expand political rights step by step from the middle class in order to make political life more vigorous and fruitful, and in an orderly and peaceful way to interest the lower classes in public affairs. 2. To make the material and intellectual fate of these classes the principal object of concern of the legislators. . . ."

Hereto must be included first of all the assimilation of tax burdens and abolition of all tax privileges, "in a word to assure to the poor man complete legal equality and comfort, which are compatible on the whole with individual rights to property and the inequalities arising therefrom. . . ."[99]

The citizens should be drawn by political rights into public life and by economic rights into the economic order. Tocqueville's basic idea, that the general structure of the republic and cooperation with equal rights within society in politics and the economy would induce the citizens to identify themselves with their institutions,[100] was valid for the public sphere; but the citizens must also have the tangible experience of equal rights and equal opportunities.

In a letter to Dufaure, Tocqueville proposed a reform of the French tax system, which would unburden the poor and impose more on the affluent,[101] and he wrote to Madame Swetchine that a more equal distribution of wealth and rights should be the most important goal of politicians.[102]

Tocqueville's reservation about the Socialists did not stem from rejection of the equality they were demanding, but from their tendency to provide more powers to the central government for the sake of equality. "I want . . . , equality in politics to consist in the fact that all are equally free and not, as is so often nowadays understood, all equally subject to one master."[103] The leveling of inequality of conditions, which must be vigorously pursued for reasons of honesty and justice, thus became an essential goal of politics, which also was politically prudent,[104] if this goal was not to be conceded to the centralists alone.

Until 1848 Tocqueville took pains in practical politics to go his own way. He busied himself with social questions, investigated problems of mutual insurance companies, addressed unjust tax burdens, and considered expansion of political rights. But he held himself apart from the Socialists because of their ideological foolishness. The Revolution of 1848, which brought into the foreground the socialistic ideas heretofore secretly agitating the citizens, put Tocqueville in a difficult situation.

On one side he was struggling against the socialistic efforts of the Left, while at the same time he allied himself on the other side with the opponents of socialism, who, as he imputed to the Socialists, showed themselves to be equally ardent exponents of a centralized order. His hostility to the Socialists caused him to seek the alliance. "Perhaps," he wrote to Beaumont, "the great number of Socialist votes will cause . . . all men who want to oppose the flood that threatens us to feel the honorable desire to unite and will move them to the decision finally to lay aside all the petty personal passions dividing them."[105] Tocqueville thought he had rediscovered in socialism the centralism and the yearning for an all-embracing and all-regulating administration of the *ancien régime* in a new disguise. He declared before the Constitutional National Assembly that socialism was the institution of a still broader power of the *ancien régime* under another name and another government, while attacking this political movement as an "energetic, continual, and excessive appeal to the material passions of men." Socialist policy was a direct or indirect but constant attack on private property, to which they ascribed all evils in the world, while all the time distrusting freedom of the spirit and the individual. The Socialists would make the state and government "masters, teachers, and trainers" of all men.[106]

Tocqueville's quarrels with the Socialists, which, it seems to me, prove first of all a partial misapprehension of the decentralizing ideas of French Socialists[107] and display his obvious prejudice,[108] stand in strange contradiction to the real objectivity with which he regarded the future of socialism.[109]

In actual fact it appears that his craving for great disputes that he hoped would lead to the formation of large political parties caused him after the Revolution of 1848 to forget all his differences with the conservative groups. It appears that a great liberal-conservative party opposing the Socialists was the object of his desires.

PROJECTED CONSTITUTIONS

"I am free," wrote Tocqueville in December 1848 to Paul Clamorgan, his agent in his electoral district, "from any feeling of affection or hate for the royal or imperial races, of any kind. . . . I have in my mind a definite ideal of a political society to the realization of which I have worked my whole life long, in vain till now. The rulers always seemed to me to be instruments which one had to employ or not employ, according to whether they might harm or further my work."[110]

His love for a free society made him argue all questions of the dynasty most cautiously. He cared less for the question of which family would rule, than for what rights and powers the government and parliament, the central administration and local institutions had, and how they would harmonize with France's traditions and customs for the sake of stable relationships.

France's geopolitical position made a strong central authority essential for this country. For this reason Tocqueville supported the monarchy under Louis Philippe before the Revolution of 1848. France had to become accustomed to continuity, and develop and foster traditions; this was more important for Tocqueville than the question whether he regarded the bourgeois king as a good ruler. Likewise in 1851 Tocqueville was for a revision of the constitution to allow to Louis Napoleon a further term in office as president of the republic, which would prevent the threatened *coup d'etat* and give the French time to consolidate orderly customs in the republic. "In my eyes, all constitutional forms are only more or less complete means," the goal is freedom,[111] and this in France required a relatively strong central power to protect the country externally against other states. But, declared Tocqueville to his friend Eugène Stoffels, "I want this central power to have a clearly delineated sphere of authority." Parliamentary control of the government is as necessary for this delimitation as a strong independent sphere for local and regional governing bodies. "Regional freedoms must be very extensive."[112]

Tocqueville was guided by the insight that local political institutions would accustom the citizens to interest themselves in their own public affairs. This promotes the citizens' initiative, consciousness, and ability to act. So the strong central government and decentralized local politics would complement each other. "I am most deeply convinced," he wrote, "that there will never be tranquillity and order if we do not succeed in joining them together."[113]

In the Constitutional Commission of 1848, in which, following the final overthrow of the monarchy, the issue was only "whether we will have a good or bad republic,"[114] Tocqueville strove to effectuate rights of self-government; but the great party of order that had been organized because of the apparent threat of socialism, included others than liberals of Tocqueville's new kind. And so the centralistic model of bureaucratic politicians won out again.[115] The republic, too, remained strongly guided by the central government. In his *Recollections*, Tocqueville resignedly concluded that "in France there is only one thing that we cannot make: a free government; and only one that we cannot destroy: centralization."[116]

His opposition to centralization in France and his efforts for decentralization in politics were no whim, as any reader of *Democracy in America* and *The Old Regime* knows. His attitude toward the question of centralization of administration was not a monomania like that of his colleague Lamennais whose thinking was so completely fixed on the concept of decentralization "that the whole structure collapsed, when one thought was removed."[117] Tocqueville looked upon decentralization as a tool to draw citizens more directly into politics, to make them experienced in the practice of political dealing, in order to take them out of their private existence. Local politics could succeed in "reviving political life everywhere, . . ."[118] and this goal of involving citizens in politics played a decisive role even before 1848, above and beyond the debates on decentralization, in the line of argument of the deputy from Valognes.

The domination of opinions

Decentralization in politics was not a goal that Tocqueville considered worth the effort for its own sake. Instead, local politics would train citizens in the love of freedom and accustom them to it, and provide them the needed practical prudence for freedom. Furthermore, the practical implementation of political rights was "the most powerful and perhaps the only means that we still possess of interesting men in the welfare of their country . . ."[119]

Tocqueville saw that, after the loss of natural patriotism, participation in politics was a significant means to draw citizens out of their privatistic individualism. As deputy, Alexis de Tocqueville wanted to pursue this second aim by making the citizens participants in public debates. His criticism of the government's policies culminated in the thesis that the government paid little attention to evoking in the citizens the passions of unselfishness, love of country, and devotion, and activating them in the cause of the nation. Heated disputes over the right policies for the welfare of France, he argued, would catch up all citizens in the political process and induce them to identify themselves with the opinions of their representatives. The result would be integration of the citizens in politics and not individualism and withdrawal into private life.

But the government refused to take this course. Its goals were stability and tranquillity at home and in foreign policy. It seemed that Guizot considered this was the sole course of action to tranquilize a country completely confused by revolutions, wars, and Restoration. He seemed to fear that any heated clash of opinions would only reawaken the revolutionary passions of the French and threaten to lead again to chaos. Hence, the government's policy was characterized by suffocation of all political life. It was just this that Tocqueville deplored. "You say that political passions are disappearing; yes, but add to that they are political passions of every kind," was how he attacked the government in 1844. "You say that bad political ideas are being renounced, and I, I say to you that also good ones are being renounced. Undoubtedly, the bad passions, the passions which give birth to persistent revolutions of every kind, the passions of violence, of anarchy, of popular tyranny, these passions are doubtless dying out. But, gentlemen, I ask you, the grand passions, the passions for freedom, for unselfishness, love of country, the desire to dedicate one's self to glory and the country's grandeur, which constituted the life and glory of the French Revolution; these passions, I ask you, have they not also died out? . . ."

In the decline of all passions, Tocqueville recognized the spreading of indifference, dangerous for the country because official policy obviously did not promote participation and left the field free for others. In the Chamber he declared: "You say the nation is calm; I say it sleeps. Believe you me, a great nation sleeps to no one's advantage. Its awakening should be feared by the whole world and from that awakening new revolutions can come forth."[120]

Tocqueville's anxiety appears understandable in relation with his reflections on the fantasizing of revolutionary dreamers. He feared and observed that the citizens were not being drawn into politics. Owing to its reduction to the rulers' interests, political reality did not mold the thinking of the French. It remained private, and in case of potential new revolutions, these private dreams would decide the course of events more than actual political problems. In order to avoid this danger, Tocqueville wanted to be sure that public politics would be so structured that the French would be drawn out of their private interests and would consciously take part in the life of the nation. This appeared possible by means of debates on principles and political directions. These debates would be effective if the heroic passions of the great Revolution could be evoked in the French; patriotism, self-sacrifice, and unselfishness.

For this reason Tocqueville felt it was desirable that parties, political groups, and public debates be founded on opinions as to policy and not just for questions of private advantage of this or that policy. Certainly, the phenomenon of particular interests had always excited, he declared; yet the critical and novel characteristic of Guizot's policy lay in the fact that the supplementary common interests that would otherwise constantly appear were made to disappear by the government's policy.[121]

If one compares this criticism particularly with the passages in the second volume of *Democracy in America*, one recognizes that in both instances Tocqueville is fighting against the same evil. It is the individualistic withdrawal of citizens out of politics, the reduction of the relationship of the citizens to society solely to economic interests, and the government's paternalistic attitude, which takes away responsibility from citizens, thereby acquires a monopoly of political action, and fosters an unpolitical withdrawal of the citizens. Tocqueville fought against the destruction of political life by a corrupt government interested only in tranquillity and order.

Analysis of Tocqueville's speeches in parliament during the July Monarchy shows that his critical disputation with "individualism" led him to seek in the French context another solution than that in *Democracy in America*.

In each case, Tocqueville saw that the citizen's withdrawal into private life and the economy was a dangerous occurrence; in the parliament of the *juste milieu*, however, there were no debates on constitutional issues on the agenda. Thus, the criticism of the deputy from Valognes was shifted more to attacks on the attitude of the government fostering individualism, and to the demand that the nation must resurrect its unity by strengthening the political passions that had become an integral part of the national character in the Revolution of 1789.

Tocqueville's attitude was entirely logical but not without problems. So long as one is prevented by centralization and bureaucratization of national policy from changing basic modes of thought (*moeurs*), one cannot change individualism by habituation to the practice of politics. The only way to fight against the withdrawal from politics was to awaken the passions for unselfishness, self-sacrifice, and patriotism.

Foreign policy

Since, however, the government's policy in internal politics had replaced controversial opinions with particular interests, public debates were mainly directed to the realm of foreign policy. "Public life seems to have withdrawn from domestic politics in order to tread the stage of foreign policy and establish itself there. I, myself, find it easy to explain this occurrence. If one replaces opinions with interests, disperses parties, if one atomizes politics, I dare to say, ruins the nation's regard for itself, if one despoils domestic politics of its grandeur, you have necessarily . . . thrust it into foreign policy. This was unavoidable, for the political life of a free people has to be played out somewhere."[122]

Tocqueville went along with this shift of the public debate to the field of foreign policy. In this connection, his aim in domestic politics on which he based his turning to foreign policy was not without significance. His concern, as we said, was to maintain and rekindle the heroic passions the French had displayed in the Revolution. The citizens ought to love their country, be ready for sacrifice, and not think only of self-interest.

Patriotism, self-sacrifice, and unselfishness, however, are not always, in every case, virtues. It depends on which goals they are subject to. One can unselfishly support the operations of a band of robbers; one can provide self-sacrifice for senseless goals; and patriotism can produce fervor in a citizen for a campaign of conquest, if this enhances the power and prestige of the beloved fatherland.

This means that these passions, which can produce extremely beneficial effects in the internal affairs of a country in certain situations, can produce completely different effects in foreign policy in certain situations—and also in internal affairs under certain circumstances. A country may arrive at a situation that, in order to foster national spirit for the sake of its internal order, may then impel it to great power ventures abroad.

Tocqueville took this dangerous course of playing with the fire of nationalistic passions. In the parliamentary debate in 1840 over the decay of the Ottoman Empire,[123] he demanded a French share in the new arrangements, and if necessary that Thiers, still in office, should risk war for it. Concurrently, he wrote to the premier: "There is only one way to prevent war, and that is to give the impression that one is determined to wage it."[124]

Even before, in his first important speech in parliament on 2 July 1839, he articulated his design for a great power policy for France. After expressing his hope that the existing monarchy might long endure, he declared he was convinced "that it will not long continue if the idea were allowed to penetrate the French spirit that we, this nation, which was formerly so strong, so grand, and which has accomplished such great things, which has intervened in all affairs of the world, can no longer intervene in anything . . . that everything takes place without her. . . ."

Tocqueville ended his speech with these words: "I say, if this belief should ever lodge itself in the heart of this proud and excitable nation . . . that would be worse than the loss of twenty battles, for that belief would ineluctably sooner or later bury the monarchy itself under the ruins of our national honor."

France, as the most progressive nation in Europe and the nation with a great past, must not decline to the level of a second-rate European nation-state. Both in the Orient question,[125] and the question of British control of maritime commercial shipping,[126] Tocqueville always demanded an independent French foreign policy. The main object of his attack on Guizot in office from the autumn of 1840 on, was the latter's policy of close collaboration with Great Britain, the *entente cordiale*.

Two considerations leading to close collaboration with England determined Guizot's foreign policy: (1) France was to be brought out of the isolation into which it had fallen as a result of the revolution of 1830, rejected by the conservative European Powers; and (2) The unstable French domestic condition compelled the country and its government to refrain from any experiments in foreign policy, since a tense situation or a possible war would lead to renewed collapse in internal politics.

Both considerations justified France's close collaboration with the English, a collaboration that Guizot pursued through thick and thin, making France a junior partner in the alliance in view of Britain's great power status, and subordinated his policy to the wishes and interests of the British.

The criticism of the opposition was heatedly focused exactly on this fact. The government was pursuing the policy of alliance with England in order not to incur a war, or even a state of tension with England, under any circumstances. Consequently, it was prepared to sacrifice if necessary French sovereign rights and interests. And what it sacrificed at the same time was national pride and French self-respect, a policy causing domestic political life and self-respect of the French to languish.[127]

Not that Tocqueville advocated war against England. It was just that he saw a distinct conflict of interests between France and the British: "Everywhere we want to take a step, whether it is in trade or industry, we encounter the interests of England, which are diametrically opposed to ours."[128] And so long as France repeatedly made clear that she wanted to avoid conflicts in foreign policy with the British and any military confrontation, she would have to bow before the wishes of the London government. With a nation which needs must be not only powerful, but all-powerful, a close and effective friendship is possible only on one condition. This is, to renounce all things in which the other wants to be all-powerful."[129]

Tocqueville demanded that the government must be prepared to a greater extent to stand up for its own interests, even militarily if necessary. Only this readiness would change the aura of the alliance and lend more weight to French wishes and aims. As early as 1840, Tocqueville articulated, in the debate on the Orient question,[130] the thought that one's full weight could be brought to bear in foreign affairs only if one made explicit a readiness to wage war, a debate in which the opposition demanded a strong French influence in the new arrangements in this part of the world. Tocqueville also made clear what he and the whole opposition understood by French interests and French tasks in world politics. "Do you know, then, what is going on in the Orient? A whole world is changing, in this gigantic area from the banks of the Indus to the coast of the Black Sea all societies are tottering, religions are weakening, nationalities are vanishing, lights are going out, the Asiatic world is vanishing, and in its place we see the European world gradually arising. The Europe of our days is pressing into not only a tiny tip of Asia, as did Europe in the time of the Crusades; it is pressing in from all sides, from north, south, east, and west." Europe was starting to develop and subdue Asia. "Do you believe then that a nation which wants to remain great can be present at such a drama without taking a part in it? Do you believe we should allow two European Powers to seize this gigantic inheritance unpunished? Yes, sooner than endure all this, I would say to my country with energy and conviction: let us wage war."[131]

NATIONALISM

Tocqueville's political standpoint in foreign policy questions plainly shows that he did not remain untouched by the questionable aspects of political passions. He knew, of course, that "patriotism is frequently a mere extension of individual selfishness,"[132] is not *per se* a virtue; yet his involvement in French foreign policy does not always show he recognized the distinction.

The actual or supposed interests of France as a European great power determined the actions of French Foreign Minister Alexis de Tocqueville in suppressing a republican uprising in Rome in 1849 by a French expeditionary corps;[133] the republicans in Rome had to concede the reestablishment of papal power in order to prevent an increase in Austrian influence.[134]

In the Roman affair, Tocqueville was less an initiator and more an administrator of an estate and unwilling executor of a failed intervention policy for which he was not responsible. But in the formulation and defense in parliament of French colonial policy, he played an appreciably more explicit and dubious role. Tocqueville propagated and supported a French colonial and imperial policy extending to suppression of other nations.

IMPERIALISM AND COLONIALISM

With this conclusion we encounter a questionable area, colonialism and imperialism, which decided like nothing else the
foreign policy of the European great powers in the nineteenth
century.

When one looks at the foreign policy of European nation-
states and the Russian Empire in the nineteenth century, of
leagues, alliances, reciprocal influence, dependencies, and national prestige, one sees that the foreign policy goals toward
non-European political societies are shunted aside completely.
The non-Europeans are not equal partners, but subjects of
the struggle for power of the Europeans. Russians, British,
and to lesser extent France, quarrel among themselves for influence in the collapsing Ottoman Empire, in the territories
bordering the Mediterranean, for commercial routes to India,
and for trade privileges in Africa and India, snatched less from
Asians and Africans than from other Europeans.

The European colonialism movement, which brought
mainly French and English as settlers in Africa, and imperialism, which drove the nation-states of Europe to a division
of the earth into "zones of influence," were caused by the desire of Europeans to dominate.

The essence of colonialist and imperialist foreign policy is
not characterized by the desire to correct frontiers, by defen-
sive alliances, or other classical goals of foreign policy, but
by the certain knowledge of the Europeans that they were
superior and the desire to transform this superiority into dominion.

The colonialist and imperialist movement seized France,
too, and Alexis de Tocqueville was as much guided by the
desire that his fatherland should rule other peoples, as most
European politicians in the nineteenth century. His concepts
of French policy in Algeria as well as his conception of
French policy on the slaves in the French colonies demonstrate that Tocqueville was not only convinced of the superi-

ority of European-American civilization, he wanted to transpose this superiority into dominion.

SLAVERY

The beacons of the American and French Revolutions were the first political and spiritual zeniths of a development in the course of which the European and American civilization brought forth new forms of political freedom and civic equality. The complicated and graduated relations of dependency of the rural inhabitants, bourgeois, aristocrats, and rulers—serfdom, bondage, inherited subjection, and so on—were entirely replaced by liberal forms of intercourse in which all citizens were treated equally under the law. One legal institution, however, remained: there was slavery in the French colonies as in the southern states of the United States of America. People, who like objects were the property of other people, who could be sold, rented, given, misused, exploited, abused—in short, were subject to the caprice of their masters. The new republics of the free and equal were also republics of slave owners. The shame of slavery which belied the talk of equality and justice, just as the existence of slaves and slave owners unmasked the talk of human rights and citizens' rights as empty phrases, obviously did not escape the notice of Tocqueville, the traveler in America and later member of parliament.

His attitude and actions concerning the legal institution of slavery are quite clear. Tocqueville not only described and criticized the evil of slavery in his book on America,[135] as an active politician he used his best efforts to support and promote the fight against the inhuman institution.[136]

Together with Beaumont Tocqueville joined the Association for Abolition of Slavery in 1835,[137] and pursued this goal in parliament,[138] just as he espoused liberation of the slaves in a series of newspaper articles.[139]

In a keen analysis, Tocqueville recognized that slavery uprooted the slaves, made expendable objects of humans, robbed them of a permanent social environment, and left them no place on earth except the house of their owner. "The Negro of the United States has lost even the remembrance of his country; the language which his forefathers spoke is never heard around him; he abjured their religion and forgot their customs when he ceased to belong to Africa, without acquiring any claim to European privileges. But he remains halfway between the two communities, isolated between two races; sold by the one, repulsed by the other; finding not a spot in the universe to call by the name of country, except the faint image of a home which the shelter of his master's roof affords."[140] Alienated and without social status, the American slave lives without a secure family, whose members may be torn apart by sale, with a frightful sense of submission which astonishes even his oppressor. "Violence made him a slave, and the habit of servitude gives him the thoughts and desires of a slave; he admires his tyrants more than he hates them, and finds his joy in the servile imitation of those who oppress him."[141] The psychic condition of the slave is the second scandal, because through violence and habituation, belief in the actual superiority of his masters and his own inferiority has become second nature for the oppressed.[142] This intensified his state of submission.

Tocqueville's radical criticism of slavery, oppression, and subjugation of the Africans, which appears so similarly in the thoughts and conclusions of radical American Negroes and anti-colonialist thinkers,[143] is the result of conclusions that were certainly fortified by conversations with his friend, Gustave de Beaumont.[144]

So it is no wonder that the reflections of the French noble centered on the question of the consequences and problems that abolition of slavery would bring, how abolition could be hastened and directed in an orderly manner, and what this would mean for the whole of society. Abolition of slavery in itself was not at all any subject for discussion. It was taken by him for granted; he was only interested in the ways and means to reach this goal. The issue, Tocqueville wrote in 1839 in the report on the deliberation of the parliamentary committee on abolition of slavery in the French colonies, was no longer to examine whether slavery is pernicious or not, but only "when and how it is sensible to terminate it."[145] The sole question then posed was how one could bring about a sensible and reasonable, that is, a controlled transition of the slaves to freedom.[146]

Already in the first volume of *Democracy in America*, Tocqueville had stated that the real social problem of slavery would not disappear with abolition of the institution.[147] For the slaveholders had deep-seated prejudices that would be much more difficult to change, reduce, and replace by other ways of thinking and viewing than the creation of juridical equality. "There is a natural prejudice that prompts men to despise whoever has been their inferior long after he has become their equal; and the real inequality that is produced by fortune or by law is always succeeded by an imaginary inequality that is implanted in the manners of the people."[148] And after juridical abolition of inequality, the significantly tougher prejudices, from which the right of slavery lives, must be addressed. "I see slavery in retreat; the prejudice from which it sprang remains unshaken."[149]

Yet Tocqueville also knew that beyond the barriers erected by prejudices which would separate masters and freedmen there was another cause of the division of society into two classes.

In the same year in which the first part of *Democracy in America* appeared, he wrote a sociopolitical research study for the Société Royale Académique of Cherbourg in which he noted the greater freedom and the higher moral state of the French rural population in the twelfth century, despite the comparable situation of these people to "the slaves of our colonies."[150] Both groups were securely provided for by their masters, enjoyed peaceful expectations for the future, which they did not shape, and a purely corporeal happiness which was hardly comprehensible in later times. The difference in the way of life of masters and rural people was caused by a division of society into two categories of people, "those who tilled the soil without owning it, and those who owned the soil without tilling it."[151]

In other words, Tocqueville knew that exclusion from owning land puts people into a situation similar to that of slaves, in spite of all other freedoms. They cannot determine their own destiny, since they depend on the means of production in the possession of others. In view of this, the proposals Tocqueville made for the orderly liberation of the slaves are not so unexceptionable as appears from a purely juridical view of the goal of granting the rights of free men to the people held as slaves in the French colonies of Guadeloupe, Martinique, and Guiana.

However much Tocqueville supported the aim of a legal liberation of the slaves, the French plantation owners' control over the way of life and working of the freed Negroes was not to be given up. The reason for this was that the Negroes in the colonies were required as a labor force after liberation.

The economy of the French overseas colonies was not only directed toward the requirements of the mother country, but it was controlled by French planters and sugar manufacturers. In order for the colonies to be able to continue to supply France uninterruptedly with their products, the white ruling class in Guadeloupe, Martinique, and Guiana had to have a sufficient labor force at their disposal on the plantations and in the sugar factories.

But the liberation of the slaves in the colonies of the British Empire had shown that the former slaves were not at once prepared to be workers for their former masters. The English had granted to the freed slaves the houses they were living in at the time, as well as small plots of land as their property. The result of this policy was that part of the former slaves tried to better their economic condition by working and cultivating their own plots of land, instead of selling their labor to the white landowners and manufacturers. The consequences were a dearth of laborers, rising wages, and a decline in production, and the French feared similar consequences if they gave freedom to the slaves in their colonies.[152]

For this reason it appeared necessary to the advocates of emancipation to assuage the fears of the slave owners as to a loss of labor forces.

"If one thinks it is essential for the exploitation of colonial production and the continuing presence of the white race in the Antilles that the freed Negro will continue to provide his labor to the plantation owners, one obviously cannot give him a property on which he can easily make a living.if he works solely for his own needs."[153] Therefore, the slaves had to be paid wages even before final liberation, for in this manner, they would learn to know the advantages of free wage labor; they would decide on the use of their income and consequently value work itself.[154] The formulation of these conclusions to which Tocqueville subscribed as *rapporteur* of a parliamentary committee was designed to induce a hesitant government to act in the question of emancipation of the slaves. In the discussion of the way emancipation was to be carried out, most attention is paid to the interests of the plantation owners, as is easily understandable in view of the political aim of the report. The owners, not the slaves, were to receive subsidies after emancipation, so that they could pay the Negroes freed from slave status.[155]

Specifically, final liberation of the slaves would be prepared by a transition period, during which the Metropole for its part would enact legislation regarding the slaves, "who would first become accustomed, and if necessary forced, to accept the diligent and manly customs of freedom."[156] The transitional legislation should make the slaves familiar with working as dependents for wages.

Tocqueville expanded on this last thought on transitional legislation to give the former slaves practice in living as free wage laborers in a series of articles in the newspaper *Le Siècle*.[157] Instead of a transition period with complicated special laws and numerous control measures, Tocqueville proposed in 1843 "a simpler, clearer, and perhaps more effective" measure: severe enforcement of existing laws against vagabondage (that is, the former slaves should be prevented from changing their residence too often) and a prohibition for Negroes to buy or possess land for a specific number of years.[158] He argued that also in France a laborer was unable to buy land, and "it is not at all a natural and necessary consequence of freedom that the Negroes in the colonies should be instantly transformed from the status of slaves to that of landowners. Such a thing had never been seen in civilized societies."[159]

The plan is very clear. The former slave owners were to have for a fixed time a monopoly of landowning, that is, of the means of production. That would compel the former slaves to become accustomed to selling their labor, instead of becoming free farmers.

ESTABLISHING A NEW ARISTOCRACY

Just as obviously the abolition of slavery was no longer a subject for debate, or whether it should take place, but only how it should be carried out, Tocqueville and the opponents of slavery obviously thought that a white ruling class should guide society in the French colonies. The white landowners and sugar manufacturers should be put in a position to control in society the mass of former slaves and people without land through their landownership rights (linked until 1848 to political rights). Unspoken in Tocqueville's proposals for an orderly liberation of the slaves was the concept of a dual race society in which the whites would assume the predominant role of an economic aristocracy, in which the former slaves would have the same place in society as the rural and growing industrial proletariat had in Europe.

The unspoken concept of a European aristocracy that would organize, promote, and profit from economic progress was justified by the goal of "civilizing" the non-Europeans, which for Tocqueville meant to make them "European." And the repeated insistence in the report that France's obligation was not only to bring these people to freedom, which they did not have, but also to prevent their regression into barbarism,[160] gives the impression that the committee members were clapping each other on the back for encouragement. For the aims of the training with which to combat "barbarism" were diligence and a pacific nature. At any rate, these seem to be the "virtues of freedom"[161] which European civilization was to bring to the barbarians. This signifies that in the minds of its imperalist protagonists European culture was reduced to those activities and skills with which one can control by economics and administration the outward conditions of development. This reduction, however, made the entire colonial society an enterprise guided as a whole and for each member by the principle of selfish advantage and usefulness. As a consequence, the obligations of the new aristocracy of colonial masters to the free laborers would be limited to the coldness and severity which occasioned Tocqueville's critical remarks in *Democracy in America*.[162] The committee consoled the white settlers losing their property rights in slaves with the thought that it might even be cheaper to have their fields cultivated by a small number of wage laborers. Each settler would be freed from the care for unproductive slaves, who would no longer have to be fed by him.[163]

The unspoken aim of a mixed society of white masters who train their free, black wage laborers in the helpful virtues of diligence and skill in calculating personal advantage shows through in Tocqueville's ideas of ways and means to free the slaves in the colonies. What could be adduced as a reason in this connection, the tactical objective of the deputy from Valognes, to provoke the least possible resistance to the overriding aim of abolishing slavery,[164] is contradicted by another facet of Alexis de Tocqueville's political views. He was a supporter of an active imperialistic policy for France and of the colonial subjection and settlement of Algeria. His support for French policy in Algeria clearly indicates that Tocqueville's concepts of a white rule over non-Europeans go beyond what could be justified by tactical considerations.

INEQUALITY

Imperialism, colonialism, and slavery, at first glance completely different phenomena, are alike in that at any given time other nations or people are not considered and treated as equals. Slavery, like European imperialism and colonialism, is based on a feeling of superiority and a derived claim to domination and leadership by Europeans over people who have not been stamped with European-Atlantic civilization.

This European feeling of superiority has specific reasons. Western civilization has in fact developed a degree of superiority from the pragmatic standpoint by application of modern discoveries and technologies in natural science, by the development of modern weapons techniques, and by the application of efficient methods of organization, which in comparison with other civilizations makes possible a more productive economy, significantly more effective forms of organization, and armaments for military units. This was the prerequisite for the conquests and violent rule of broad areas of the earth, for the exploitation and taking possession of extensive regions and populations, and for the subjection of the inhabitants of these regions.

The subjects were robbed of their identity by imperialism, colonialism, and slavery, and subject to exploitation and direction by the Europeans. Deciding their own fate, either for slaves or for peoples subjected to colonial rule, was out of the question.

Nevertheless, aside from the above-mentioned similiarities, there are substantial differences between slavery and colonial rule. While colonial rule does rob a subject people of the political and economic rights of determining its destiny, slavery goes much further: the slave is denuded of all rights, is treated as a commodity, and is subjected to the direct whim of his owner.

However much emancipation of the slaves was an urgent necessity for Tocqueville on purely humanitarian grounds, he did not pursue his train of thought to its conclusion. A purely juridical freeing of the slaves with concomitant maintenance of economic control and political rule by the Europeans in the colonies would continue the condition of lack of political and economic freedom, despite the liberation of individuals of the affected peoples as members of society. Slaves would become subjects.

On humanitarian grounds, Tocqueville wanted to abolish the juridical institutions of civic inequality. But the equality he thought worth striving for took in for non-Europeans only equality of rights of the physical person. There was no question of political rights of self-determination, or of economic and social equality of conditions. Tocqueville's ideas, flowing toward the imposition of economic conditions on the legally freed slaves that would keep them dependent on European masters, become more explicit in his attitude toward colonialism. In the specific question of the young French colony in Algeria, there was no talk of equal rights, aside from complete equality in conditions of economic opportunity.

3
Algeria

We need not be concerned in detail with the various campaigns by which France subjugated those North African regions that were later to bear the name of Algeria or with the various phases of these campaigns of conquest.

A silly incident on the diplomatic level, intrigues at the French court, and perhaps the desire of King Charles X to alleviate his precarious domestic situation by activities abroad are the visible causes for sending a French expeditionary corps to North Africa early in 1830, which officially was to reestablish French honor. It cannot be ignored that France stumbled into the Algerian adventure without ever having seriously debated the aims, sense, and methods of subjugation of the population inhabiting the North African territories.

After initial military successes the French army settled down in North Africa and conquered the whole country in several phases lasting until 1847.[1] The vague aims of the first expedition, the interruption of a consequent policy by the July Revolution of 1830, and also the relatively little interest evinced by responsible authorities in Paris in the Algerian question brought it about that the conquest of the peoples in the territory of Algeria bore all the earmarks of an unplanned policy never seriously thought out. At first, the harbors on the North African coast were desired; then, it was a matter of preventing British influence; later, the harbors had to be secured by hinterlands and the inhabitants were to receive the blessings of European civilizations; and at times, the goal was simply to increase French power and French-controlled territory.

For students of France's Algerian policy up to 1852 the lack of aims and conception of this undertaking is horrifying. France's conquest of this North African country has all the traits of an irrational action, obvious from the beginning. The purpose and reason for the enterprise were never really presented, and consequently its goals remained hazy, irrational, and obscure. Debate and the enterprise itself were determined by means of the conquest and military pressure, and the result was that the declared goals and justification of the French presence in North Africa changed according to the advance of French troops and the civilians following them.[2]

This aimlessness, for its part, had a horrible effect on the manner with which the conquest was carried out. Commanding generals in Algeria like Bugeaud or La Moricière determined France's Algeria policy probably more strongly than any single responsible politician or government, and the policy reflected that spirit. The military, left free of any political guidance, terrorized, plundered, and destroyed the country and subjected the whole enterprise to thinking of military goals. The conquest became an end in itself, and the means these goals demanded were applied with a brutality that included plundering, burning the food of the inhabitants, murder, massacre, and terror. What was to be conquered and subjugated, in this state of affairs, was more a question of military calculation than one of political deliberation. As the conquest and subjugation progressed, they became desirable in metropolitan France.[3]

The goals of the conquest

The changes in the goals of the French government's policy were subjects for Tocqueville's attention. In 1837 he wrote in a newspaper article that the goal of the French could not be to subject the Kabyle tribes militarily.[4] Neither the great military exertions nor the prospects of success made this seem worth the effort. The attractiveness of modern civilization would in the long run bring about an automatic adaptation by the Kabyles to the French way of life.[5] At the same time, there were a number of Arab tribes that should be directly ruled by the French. "Yet the majority even of these tribes should be ruled only indirectly and influenced. The whole purpose of our present care should be to live in peace with those Arabs whom we cannot presently hope to govern. . . ."[6] On these, too, the superiority of European culture would in the long run exercise a sufficient integrative attraction.[7] Only in that portion of the country where French and Arabs lived side by side did "our security as well as our honor require" the exercise of direct power and rule without intermediary authority.[8]

In May 1841, Tocqueville toured Algeria as a deputy. The notes he made at the time show his vacillation between the possible goals of the French presence in North Africa. On 29 May he noted: "It is probable that we will have a war if we seriously try to colonize with Europeans. It would be better to exploit the country in Egyptian fashion, that is, through natives, but for the benefit of the government." If France would refrain from threatening the Kabyle tribes in their territories, "we would achieve that they will come to us and furnish all sorts of things."[9] Two days later he expressed doubts. "It seems very clear to me that the moment we try to use our control in the province of Constantine to colonize it, peace would end and our control would be in doubt. On the other hand, where does control lead us, if not to colonization?"[10] He acknowledges the possibility of trade relations, "if one is wise enough to abstain from all actions *vis-à-vis* the Kabyles which give the Kabyles cause to fear that we will attack them," only to ask, "but will we always have this wisdom? I doubt it."[11] Tocqueville very obviously was pondering the sense of France's presence in Algeria. He was vacillating between a policy aimed at trade and indirect influence, and a policy of colonization, which he recognized as unwise, that would lead to war. It is important that these notes were made incidentally; they contain only sudden thoughts and ideas, and formulate no fixed policy. After returning to France, Tocqueville began to put his ideas and experiences in order. In October 1841, he wrote an extensive draft manuscript, which expressed quite other ideas and goals. The recognition that the tribes in the hinterlands were hostile to the French presence now led to the conclusion that the partial colonization must be secured by complete French rule in Algeria.[12]

Now the maintenance of national prestige determined every consideration of French specific measures in Algeria. Although in 1837 for Tocqueville France's goal in Algeria was "gradual establishment of a mixed-race society, which would erect a great monument to the glory of our fatherland on the coast of Africa,"[13] three years later the mastery of Algeria had become a necessary demonstration of French claims to great power status. "I do not believe that France can seriously consider leaving Algeria"; so begins the draft of his work on Algeria. But the justification no longer deals with North Africa, but with the impression of weakness that a French withdrawal would give to other countries. France could only leave Algeria if it undertook "great things in Europe," which would assure its rank among the first powers.[14] Now the conquest of Algeria is justified primarily from military and foreign policy standpoints; it was a question of consolidating France's position in the Mediterranean by ports in North Africa and the importance of France in Europe.[15]

No longer should the situation in North Africa determine the French advance, but the situation in Europe. It followed that the complete conquest must proceed rapidly for "so long as this task continues, our capacity to act in the world is limited and the arms of France are as if paralyzed, a condition which must be rapidly ended, as much for our security as for our honor."[16] Only complete mastery of the whole territory would make the French colony safe and permit the troops tied down there to withdraw.

Thus the effective application of military force in the conquest decided the conquest itself. And Tocqueville, who as late as 1837 wrote that there was no reason to believe the two races could not in time come together ("God does not prevent it; only the mistakes of men could prevent it"),[17] set down in 1842 in his notebook: "I do not believe in the possibility of a mixture of the two races."[18] The span of five years separating the two seemingly contradictory statements had actually produced so many "errors of men" preventing coexistence of Frenchmen and native inhabitants of Algeria, that Tocqueville's originally proposed goal of a mixed-race society had become impossible as a result of the means France employed to achieve it. And therefore the remaining goal of France in the Algerian undertaking was the creation of a colony of European settlers in North Africa, which had to be protected from the Algerians by French rule of the whole territory.

THE MILITARY CAMPAIGN AGAINST
THE NATIVES

Toward the end of the Algerian campaign Tocqueville stated: "One can only study barbaric peoples with a weapon in hand. We have conquered the Arabs before we got to know them."[19] And he knew very well that this "study with weapon in hand" was no normal war which France was waging. The enemy of the French was no army, no government. The enemy was the peoples and tribes of the Arabs and Kabyles,[20] whose resistance to foreign domination and the French army should be broken. The military actions of the army that, as Tocqueville noted, "seized unarmed men, women and children . . . are . . . vexing necessities . . . which any nation has to undergo to wage war against the Arabs."[21]

From 1841, when it was more and more apparent that the widespread resistance of the tribes could not be broken solely by military measures, the French General La Moricière developed a new military technique, the *razzia*,[22] adopted by most of the French army. In nocturnal surprise attacks, French troops fell on Arab tribes, shot down all resisters, stole the cattle and food reserves of the victims, who were raped, dispersed, pursued, or killed. What could not be stolen, or was useless, was burned. Whole areas were laid waste in this manner, villages and towns destroyed, trees in oases cut down, and the latter made uninhabitable. Massacres of whole tribes as well as murders of individuals, plundering, torturing, and senseless brutality were usual actions of an army without discipline,[23] that not only increased its pay by auction and sale of stolen people and objects, but more and more adopted methods that ensured self-sufficiency of the troops and also enrichment of individual soldiers.

Tocqueville rejected the brutalities occurring in this kind of warfare. The barbarity of the troops was worse than that of the enemy Arabs.[24] But his criticism was very restrained and made exception for destruction of harvests and the plundering of food supplies of Arab tribes and also the displacement of noncombatant civilians.[25] Insofar as this *razzia* system only satisfied the ambition of commanders, it was to be rejected, "but often it seems to me these *razzias* are necessary, and one would be wrong to condemn them."[26]

This military technique of attacking tribes by surprise, destroying harvests, and laying waste whole areas was designed, so he wrote, to show the Arabs that the French were irresistible in Algeria. In this way, their resistance could be broken. The enemy tribes would thus see that the leader of the Algerian resistance, Abd-el-Kader, could not protect them. "What is unbearable for an Arab tribe in the long run is not the passage of an army corps through its territory, but the proximity of mobile troops which can attack at any time by surprise."[27] Only terror against the civilian population could break the resistance and in the long run suppress support of the rebels. Consequently, Tocqueville defended even in parliament, the strategy of the commanding General Bugeaud,[28] who, like Tocqueville, compared and defended *razzias* with the cannonading and besieging of cities in Europe.[29]

THE COLONY

The methods by which the French army terrorized the Arab and Kabyle tribes until the complete subjugation under French rule could not fail to affect the prospects of coexistence of conquerors and subjects after the war. The brutality of the oppressors and the hate of the subjected, who acquired a new understanding of themselves and developed the concepts of nationalism of their new masters, rendered impossible violence-free collaboration of old and new inhabitants of Algeria.

Tocqueville was aware of the dangers of the brutality of the oppressors as well as those of the hatred of the Arabs and Kabyles, yet did not inquire as to the reasons that would expose the dubious nature of the whole French undertaking. He persisted in looking at the surface of events characterized by violence. The French soldiers in Algeria seemed to him "from the military viewpoint" worthy of admiration. But, Tocqueville wrote further, "I concede that they give me anxiety, and I ask myself what will we do with a large number of such men when they return among us." For these men, through the manner they had learned to treat other people, were accustomed to a hard, violent, partisan and crude way of governing, the expansion of which was a cause for worry.[30]

This manner of governing was also a serious problem in Algeria. In 1847 Tocqueville, as a recognized parliamentary expert on Algeria and *rapporteur* of a committee, declared that the resistance of the conquered made it seem inadvisable "to think that we can easily and in a short time succeed in eradicating the silent hate, nourished by foreign domination, in the heart of the native."[31] And so he proposed a system of rule and suppression which had nothing in common with the goal he originally espoused. There was no further talk of a mixed-race society with population groups enjoying equal rights. The settlement of Algeria by Europeans, the establishment of European villages and cities, development of agriculture and cultivation of the soil, particularly by French settlers, were goals that Tocqueville never lost sight of when he spoke of problems of establishing French rule in Algeria. "Quiet possession of the coastline and settlement of parts of the country" are the goals to be served by means of dominion over all Algerian territory.[32] That is, the decisive problem of political order in the French colony of Algeria after the conquest would be coexistence of the inimical population groups. Tocqueville no longer believed in the mixture of the two races. History, religion, laws, and the events during the conquest had created a chasm poisoning relations between the groups. "It would hardly be intelligent to believe that we could succeed in associating ourselves with the natives through a community of ideas and customs" was the crystalline manner in which he stated the conclusion of the parliamentary committee of 1847. All one could hope for was the creation of a community of interests.[33]

And this community of interests was not to be based on equal rights for the various groups. Rather, the primacy of the interests of the European settlers should be imposed on the consciousness of those affected and in the legal and property systems.

"Neither advantage nor duty require us to give our Mohammedan subjects exaggerated ideas of their importance, and we must not convince them that we are bound in all circumstances to treat them exactly as if they were our fellow citizens and equals. They know that we have a dominant position in Africa, and they understand that we will maintain it. If we should concede it today, this would only plant astonishment and confusion in their minds, and would fill them with erroneous and dangerous ideas."[34]

These subjects, conscious of not being fellow-citizens and equals, should therefore be ruled by a strict government forcing compliance with the laws,[35] which should show neither generosity nor indulgence. Not exploitation, but the interest of all groups should determine the actions of the government, which would embrace the interests of all. This, according to Tocqueville's committee, would attract the subjects to the blessings of private property, of crafts, and sedentary life, which was in their own interest.[36]

The demand for strong, overpowering government to ensure, guarantee, and if necessary, enforce, unity in the society of Algeria stemmed from the goal of colonization. The completely differently constituted groups that were to form a society were actually in a state of latent civil war. In addition, the planned strong government was not only to ensure the *status quo;* the goal of colonization made necessary a series of changes that would very largely overturn the way of life of the affected Arabs. The introduction of European private property law, the attempt to make the Arab tribes sedentary, and the attempt to induce Arabs and European immigrants to live side by side in a number of areas did indeed make essential a government with strong, overpowering compulsory force, because, at least for the Arab tribes that did not live on the coast or in cities, engaged in trading, handicrafts, or agriculture, the issue was not only dominion over the land, but their way of life.

The seminomadic Arab tribes in Algeria had no conception of European property rights to land and soil. A tribe had areas traditionally claimed by it, through which it passed, which it sometimes used for farming, on which its accompanying herds grazed, and which served its seminomadic way of life. This partially sedentary way of life of the tribes was only possible by this completely different manner of using the land, from the economic standpoint the most extensive form of land use, but from the standpoint of partially sedentary way of life, the only acceptable form of use or ownership. This meant that the introduction of European private real property law must necessarily destroy the seminomadic life of the tribes, unless all the land the tribes used was to be granted and guaranteed to them as property. Also, it was easy to induce the tribes, ignorant of European property law, to sell parts of their lands, which also led to destruction of the basis of their way of life.

This meant that the introduction of a private land tenure

system would destroy the way of life of the seminomadic Arab tribes. That is what France did.

Viewed from the European free enterprise standpoint, Algeria was a largely uninhabited and unexploited territory. The land could certainly be more profitably exploited in agriculture. Of course, more profitable use rather obviously presupposed European forms of free trade and property rights different from the concepts of the natives.

The country was already inhabited, and a minority of the parliamentary committee consequently feared that penetration by a new population would perpetuate the state of war and the inevitable destruction of the existing groups of inhabitants.[37] These fears were not shared by the committee's majority, whose analysis and proposals for the formation of Algeria show how they proposed to counter obviously difficult problems. This is especially clear in regard to the property issue.

Tocqueville knew that the chances of large-scale immigration into Algeria would stand or fall on land grants, and for him this immigration was an indispensable prerequisite for French rule. "The future of our rule in Algeria depends on one event . . . the arrival of a European population on African soil," he declared in parliament in 1846,[38] and since he took French rule to be self-evident, his thoughts centered on the question of how one could put the land at the disposal of the French government.

Already in his work in 1841, he had stated that France could become established in Algeria only if it took the land away from the tribes. In the province of Algiers, to be sure, this could be limited to those tribes "which fought against us. The measure is violent, but according to the customs of the country it is not unjust."[39] Certainly, one wanted to export European culture to Africa, but if the legal system of the subjects favored the goals of the conqueror, it would be adopted. That in Tocqueville's mind it was not a matter of the effectuation of a right becomes clear in following passages. Where the Moors own the land that should pass into the hands of the European settlers, he argues that the government should take possession of the land, "either by voluntary sale or by force," undeterred by the fact that these population groups had never undertaken hostile action against France. Of course, compensation should be given,[40] but the will and the rights of the owners must be subordinated to the goal of colonization. The Moors were inhibiting settlement, "and we have no use for them."[41]

In Tocqueville's way of thinking, the government should make itself the owner of large sections of the country "by the right of the conqueror, whether by voluntary sale or by forced expropriation."[42] The land so obtained would then be transferred according to plan to settlers for their use.[43] The same idea of centralized acquisition of land, which would be resold to settlers, turned up in the committee report of 1847.[44] France could not, of course, simply seize the land like a barbarian nation, but it did not follow that one had to abstain from possessing the land needed for colonization. Experience had shown that it was very possible to acquire the needed land by exchange of land or purchase at a cheap price. Herein appears one after the other a series of arguments, which illuminate the line of thinking of the committee majority, which included Tocqueville: (1) the existence of a problem of land ownership was denied; there was much unused land; (2) there was much publicly owned land, and this could be distributed to settlers; and (3) land presently owned by individual tribes could be at least partly taken.[45]

It was dubious enough to assert as self-evident the obvious assumption set forth under number 2, that in fact public ownership had passed to the conqueror, who, heedless of possible previous owners, could distribute it to settlers. But it is the argument on the third point that most clearly shows the attitude of the conquerors. The problem that the tribal way of life was based on entirely different legal and property concepts, was simply ignored. For reasons of time and space they did not wish to burden the Chamber with a presentation and discussion of property law in Africa. "These questions are by nature very obscure. . . ."[46]

In many regions, there was no private ownership of land at all, and in many others, "the communal ownership by the tribes is not based on any legal title, and is actually more the result of the government's toleration than a right." Therefore, concluded the committee, parliament could recognize without any concern, "that it is easier to introduce a new population in a territory which is only a communal property than in a region in which every inch of land is defended by a single owner or a single interest."[47] Moreover, it was easy to induce a tribe that had a territory too big for it and did not occupy it "to cede a part of its land, if it is guaranteed possession of the other part." It is plain that Tocqueville and the committee of the Chamber of Deputies wanted not only to introduce private real property law into Algeria, but also the concept that the previous owners and users of the land should cede a part of the land in exchange for a guarantee of the rest. However, the rest was no longer enough for a seminomadic life, and the tribes would have to adjust to the European way of life.

The destruction of the traditional system of use and ownership was an attack going to the root of the way of life and identity of the nonsedentary tribes living on Algerian soil. Introduction of private real property rights would make impossible the way of life of the free tribes and indicate another course; they would have to submit to European economic patterns and thus to the European system of division of labor.

In any case, the positions of landowner and farmer were mostly reserved for others, and so there remained for the original inhabitants and owners of the land only to prove that they were useful, "our farmers will gladly make use of the arms of the natives," and as compensation, the Europeans would give the former owners the opportunity to earn high wages.[48]

Behind the government's function of buying up and distributing the land stood unmistakably a transformation of the whole way of life of the Arab tribes, who were to be Europeanized and despoiled of their original identity. And the far-reaching proposals of the committee for reform of the administrative structure in Algeria were intended to make the communities of settlers in this enterprise more effective.[49]

COLONIZATION, JUSTICE, AND FREEDOM

Tocqueville was fascinated by the thought of colonizing Algeria. He thought that in North Africa he had discovered a territory in which his fatherland could carry out a settlement as the English had done in North America. André Jardin points out that about 1833 he even contemplated settling in Algeria with his friend Louis de Kergorlay.[50] And in fact two letters bear witness to these plans.[51] His notes on his first trip to Algeria in 1841 are full of references to America,[52] and later the committee report of 1847 refers to the American experience.[53]

The desire to colonize and the desire to change the lifestyle of the Arab tribes were firmly fixed in Tocqueville. These desires determined the perspectives of his observations.[54] But these desires themselves were never tested, discussed, or even examined as to their promise of success.

At present, we can state with fair justification that a twentieth-century European can easily draw up criticism of the fact that Tocqueville never reflected on his colonization goals and desires. The nineteenth century could hardly foresee the disaster of the collapse of its imperialist and colonialist policy. And France, like all other nations in the nineteenth century, had not been seized by the critical self-examination that causes us today to judge severely the Europeans' expansive struggle for domination. There were, of course, some critics of the undertaking at the time of the conquest of Algeria, and there can be no doubt that Tocqueville was aware of this criticism. But France never experienced a great debate on the purpose of a French colony in North Africa. André Tudesq concludes that as early as 1840 opposition to the conquest was dampened by "the fear of appearing to oppose the general will of the nation."[55] His analysis of the whole debate clearly shows that French minds were not intensely occupied with the Algerian enterprise.[56] When problems regarding Algeria were discussed in France, they were technical problems of executing the conquest, practical issues concerning the extent of settlement,[57] or questions as to conducting the war. To this extent, Tocqueville was a child of his times, wrapped up in the illusions and delusions of grandeur, convinced of the civilizing obligation of the old continent, and unshaken in his convictions by any piercing questions.

However, any admirer of Tocqueville is baffled. Why did not the author of *Democracy in America* pose the piercing questions himself? Melvin Richter correctly notes that Tocqueville's standpoint in the Algerian question cannot be reconciled with his work on America.[58] He concludes that in his studies of 1841 on Algeria, Tocqueville put his intellectual faculties at the service of an Occidental state that was determined to conquer a territory outside Europe, although he knew that conquest by a foreign power was a great evil for any society.[59]

Even though Tocqueville, in the Chamber of Deputies in 1846, opposed the ideological madness that demanded that the Arabs be wiped out, since they stood in the way of progress,[60] and although he, as *rapporteur* of the committee, rejected gradual complete expulsion of the Arab inhabitants from Algeria,[61] contradictions remain. Chevalier and Jardin arrive at the conclusion that Tocqueville regarded the Arab inhabitants of Algeria as eternally unequal to Europeans.[62] The result of the French policy of conquest had to be political and economic rule by European immigrants or, as Seymour Drescher states in larger context, a new aristocratic rule by Europeans over the original inhabitants.

"Imagine . . . an aristocracy, established through conquest, at a time not long past so that memories and traces of those events are still present in all minds. Imagine the time of conquest at a period when the conqueror already possesses all knowledge of civilization while the conquered is still half in a state of barbarism, so that the one stronger in moral power is also stronger in knowledge. . . . Give these different and unequal beings different religions, so that the nobleman not only mistrusts the people, but also hates it; that the people not only hate the nobleman, but damn him. Then give this aristocracy no reason to associate with the people, but even a special reason not to do so, in order to remain equal with the nation from which they came, from which they draw their entire strength, and of which they boast they are equals.

"Instead of giving the aristocrats a distinct motive to treat the people justly, give them a motive to suppress it, since they can rely on help from abroad, and need not fear the consequences of their tyranny. Grant this aristocracy the exclusive power to rule and to amass wealth. Prevent the people from attaining the status of aristocrats, or allow this advancement only under unacceptable conditions. It follows that the people, thrown back on themselves, designated aliens by the hostility of the upper classes, with no hope of improving their lot, will finally surrender and be content with gaining as much from the land by manifold exertions as will support life. The aristocrat on the other hand, shorn of any motive impelling humans to great and generous actions, rests on his selfishness and knowledge."[63]

This "horrible condition of society" in which the aristocracy will develop "all the mistakes and principles of oppressors" and "the people all the vices and baseness of slaves," produces, according to Tocqueville, who observed this in Ireland, "one of the most abominable" forms of government that one has ever imagined.[64]

Tocqueville's observations about the British-Anglican rule over the Catholic Irish match the French rule in Algeria point for point. Thus, Tocqueville knew precisely what was at stake when French settlement and rule in Algeria were discussed.

Why did not Tocqueville apply his knowledge of the injustice and inhumanity of foreign rule to the Algerian situation? Looking at it superficially, the question can be quickly answered. The "spirit of the times" prevented Tocqueville from considering the inhabitants of Algeria as equals. The "Eurocentrism" of the nineteenth century compelled citizens of the nation-states of our continent to look on other civilizations primarily from the viewpoint of how they could be made useful to Europe, or at best, how they could be Europeanized. The "nationalism" to which Tocqueville was subject was expansive in the nineteenth century and the general climate of opinion tended toward oppression and exploitation of non-European nations. But none of these is an explanation. "Spirit of the times," "Eurocentrism," "nationalism" are general expressions of the attitude that should be explained; they only portray it.

An economic explanation falls short. It is true that some Frenchmen made considerable fortunes in Algeria; yet for France Algeria was never a truly profitable venture, and it cannot be shown that there was any connection between colonial settler-profiteers and Tocqueville. The groups of people who profited directly or indirectly from the settling in Algeria had no political or economic importance either for France or for Tocqueville. In addition, capitalistic need for expansion found considerably greater opportunities for investment in France than in the underdeveloped colony. Besides, it would be inconceivable to attempt to unmask Tocqueville as the political exponent of economic interests.

The question remains, why did Tocqueville, knowing the evil consequences of foreign rule, propagate and support the conquest, and in part the settling and rule of Algeria by France?

My answer is: Tocqueville never applied his knowledge of the evil consequences of foreign rule to Algeria. The strange thing about his works, declarations, notes, and reports on Algeria is the peculiar unquestioning nature of these documents. Tocqueville's inquiring mind was never seriously occupied at any time with the problems of the future coexistence of Algerians and French in North Africa, if one ignores his proposals for establishing peace, which can only be seen as the prelude to settlement of parts of the territory by Frenchmen.

This failure to question, to inquire into the aim of French rule and settlement, and hence never seriously to question the sense of this aim, was caused by the exclusively French viewpoint from which Tocqueville investigated the Algerian problem. In Tocqueville's mind, Algeria was mainly a French affair, even before the successful campaigns. At first, he saw the chance for a new settlement similar to the English settlements in North America; later, he considered Algeria a principal task of the French Metropole, even "the greatest concern of the country."[65] But the order to be established in Algeria, requiring local autonomy, decentralization, and the security of law, was an order of Europeans, by Europeans, and for Europeans.[66]

Tocqueville, who in another context clearly recognizes that patriotism is "frequently only an extension of individual selfishness,"[67] who thus knew it was a matter of passion, wanted to improve the political condition of his country by mobilizing this passion in the French. The effort to mobilize the patriotic feelings of the French through the conquest of Algeria appealed to a passion in which neither the French he addressed nor Tocqueville, the appealer, paid attention to the fate of the Algerians. The sole concern was France.

With this conclusion we reach a point where the limits of Tocqueville's understanding of politics and freedom, as orator and politician, become clear.

THE LOGICAL IMPASSE IN RHETORICAL POLITICS

We have tried to demonstrate how central in Tocqueville's thinking was the search for order and a common good determining that order. The dialectical relation thus developed between love of freedom and a constitution for freedom appears necessary in connection with Tocqueville's concepts regarding French politics in Algeria, but an insufficient condition for a reasonable political order.

In his analysis of individual life reduced to reckoning usefulness, Tocqueville came up against the depraved form of rationality that is confined to the shrewd calculation of personal advantages. For him, that discredited reason as such. Tocqueville fell victim to the reduction of reason to pragmatic rationalism, which characterized seventeenth- and eighteenth-century thinking. He never speaks of that inquiring reason which characterizes the philosopher's openness, his behavior and attitude toward opinions, his speech and actions. And although in his search for a central point of order he thus developed a concept of free action, he was unable to define the criterion for specific actions through an understanding of reason, which inquires beyond intermediate goals. His abhorrence of individualistic actions guided purely by self-interest and his contempt for calculation of private economic interest were not sufficient to advance to the attitude and the way of thinking of a man shaped by reason and its openness. Tocqueville's search for order took place in an intellectual atmosphere in which the use of reason was no longer recognizable as the common and connecting intellectual activity of human existence; and hence, there arose the antithesis of interests and opinions in his interpretation of European reality.[68] Politics, he declared in criticizing the rulers of the *juste milieu*, must appeal to the citizens from the aspect of their self-interest; it had to mobilize citizens' opinions and be supported by them. Opinions are mobilized by appeals to people's passions. And consequently, Tocqueville looked for passions that could give direction and support to politics and order.

He sought a *passion* that would draw humans out of their small, circumscribed, private interests. In Tocqueville's thinking, freedom therefore became a surrender to passions. "Only freedom," he declared in 1842 in his speech to the academy, "can infuse us with those mighty and common passions which carry souls along and lead them out of themselves; . . . only it can draw our spirit out of petty thoughts . . ."[69] And in a letter to Ampère he complained about parliament. "I see only cowards who are afraid of the slightest excitement in the human heart and tell us of the dangers threatening us from passions. In my view that is idle talk. What one encounters least in our days are passions, true, strong passions which captivate and drive life on. We no longer understand how to desire, to love, or to hate. Doubt and philanthropy render us incapable of great things, whether for good or for evil, and we flutter peacefully around a lot of trivialities, none of which attracts us or repels us strongly, or gives us direction."[70] The lack of knowledge of good order, order which in the soul of the political citizen is experienced by inquiring reason and which determines his actions among his equals, thus leads to surrender to a passion, which, lacking reasonable self-control, strives to regain internal order by the goal of expansion abroad. The passionate desire to rule others, to create greatness in his own nation by rule over other nations, it seems to me, is the result of the vagueness of Tocqueville's own idea of freedom. To the extent that freedom becomes the goal of human existence and is practiced in the pursuit of the mighty passions it includes it becomes problematic. Tocqueville's sociologically correct insight, that reason can only prevail if it hits upon a passion which by chance accompanies it,[71] cannot justify the misfortune that the passion for dominion brings to other nations.

This conclusion leads beyond an analysis of Tocqueville's attitude to colonialism and imperialism.

Tocqueville appears, so to say, to be a victim of the law of human existence he expounded in his book on America, that is, the law that compels an active man "to accept general ideas without discussion,"[72] if he wants to be seriously concerned at least with a few. The insight set forth in *Democracy in America* of the capability of human beings to mirror all principles of social order and human activity, as being limited by the finiteness of human existence, is even truer for the practical politician than for the theorist of society.

Tocqueville, as practicing politician, was compelled to accept many of the prevailing opinions without thinking about them, in order to act at all. But the attitude toward other nations set forth above makes the problematic character of this procedure apparent. And just as the conclusion is right that each government is based on a consensus of opinion, so it becomes clear to the reader of Tocqueville's conception of imperial foreign policy that this says nothing regarding the quality of that type of government. It is correct "that all governments rest on opinions." Yet this only repeats the question as to the goodness and reasonableness of the opinions on which the government rests.

Tocqueville levels a justified and massive criticism against individualistic withdrawal from society and politics. But it must not be overlooked that there is still another kind of aloofness from the world of men than that of the withdrawal of the average citizen into privacy. It is the transcendence of opinions and passions through inquiring reason.

In the first part of our inquiry, we sought to demonstrate how thoroughly for Tocqueville freedom was freedom in society. The limits of this concept of freedom now become apparent. If the criterion of just order and just action remains at the level of opinions and passions and requires only that they pass beyond calculation of advantage, the question as to which passions should determine politics becomes a question of taste. Yet the mobilization of citizens by means of the "right passions" remains even in theory a question of power. But power is based on the opinions and passions of the citizens in one's own country—at best those of one's own larger sphere of civilization. This finally indicates the limit of the rhetorical concept of politics that appeals to opinions.

Tocqueville addressed his line of argument to his fellow citizens. And since Tocqueville's thinking and procedure prevented him from viewing his equals as "objects" of the investigation, he remained in the cosmos of his own civilization. Yet the citizens of Algeria were objects for him, without equal rights and certainly not equals.

The rhetorical practical manner of presentation and investigation, which seeks *in* society to instruct, convince, and win over another person, and which therefore takes his opinions and convictions seriously or tries to alter them, proves fruitful for investigation of the problems of the domestic order. It is essential for a resonable relationship with a fellow citizen. But it is insufficient, because the criteria of reasonable action and reasonable judgment cannot be found in the cosmos of the fellow citizens' opinions and passions. It is true that all governments rest on opinions, but by this conclusion human beings are not freed from the necessity to gain the criteria of their judgments and actions from insights extending beyond opinions and discursive rhetoric. Even the most heroic passions and opinions appropriate to produce them are insufficient as bases also for domestic order. The goals sought by these passions must be able to pass another test than that of the passions themselves.

Tocqueville, who regarded the rule of opinions with the greatest skepticism, but who applied this skepticism explicitly only against petty individualistic opinions, recognized that fact himself. Opposing the tyranny of the opinions of the majority, he appealed to "a general law, which bears the name of justice, . . . made and sanctioned, not only by a majority of this or that people, by a majority of mankind."[73]

4
Liberalism

Modern industrial societies of the Western liberal form are developing into a situation that makes perceptible for everyone a number of those problems which Tocqueville examines and presents. Considerations of economic efficiency, especially when they almost exclusively shape the self-perception of the governed and the governors, are not a good guide for structuring a political order. Centralization and the ensuing bureaucratization of a country's political life do not produce self-reliant citizens, who take their fate in their own hands, nor does the concentration of powers and the transfer of authority to civil servants provide an opportunity to acquire the practical wisdom that can only be learned in practice.

The problem of responsible participation of citizens in the political life of their society is easily assumed to have been solved by the democratic revolutions of the eighteenth and nineteenth centuries. The problem of political participation was removed from the agenda by the massive progress of industrialization and the struggle for shares in distributing the growing production. But initially it determined the thinking of Liberals and the Socialists who arose after them.

The general, equal, and secret voting franchise does not by a long shot make a republic out of a sovereign state, and this is an important result of Tocqueville's deliberations. In proportion as the ever increasing production figures become questionable for the citizens, the repressed problem of the citizens' freedom presents itself again, and liberalism of Tocqueville's new style again acquires importance.

The question whether the free societies of the West will succeed in reestablishing or maintaining freedom as a tangible way of life in their consciousness, in their dealings, and in political institutions is not yet decided. Will we succeed in creating democratic republics that are the concern of citizens, or are Western societies threatened with the fate of becoming completely existential welfare states in which friendly paternal bureaucracies take all responsibility from us, while we citizens applaud at periodic intervals?

Can we succeed in bringing about a rebirth of Liberal thinking above and beyond the economy?

But precisely if we answer this question positively, which is not at all certain, we have to bear in mind the limits of Liberal political thinking.

For one thing, there is the realm of industrial production, administration, and organization, neglected by Liberal thinking; yet it determines the behavior of all working citizens, and it does not easily fit institutions oriented toward freedom.

In addition, there are limits to Liberal thinking in the political realm itself. Freedom of expression, freedom of action and associated civil rights, parliamentary government, a constitution, and publicity that makes it possible for the citizen to take part in political life are the cornerstones of a Liberal order. The struggle to put these principles into practice in free societies, and the struggle to maintain and extend them is certainly the most important service of liberalism, whose special expression in the thinking of Alexis de Tocqueville and his new-style liberalism impresses and influences anyone deeply concerned over the bureaucratization and regimentation of political life in free societies. Nevertheless, the great achievements and goals of liberalism taken together set forth the conditions, and not the content, of rational human existence in society and history.

Freedom of expression permits the propagation of nonsense, and freedom to act can be used for the subjection of others.

The existence of civil rights is no guarantee for their reasonable use. Legislative bodies can also pass unjust laws. Authority set forth in constitutions can be misused by officeholders for inequitable purposes. Participation by citizens in public life does not automatically motivate citizens to strive for justice. A functioning system of communication is no guarantee that public debate is molded by reason, and not by the private interests and passions of the debaters; and public debate on politics is no guarantee of a rational outcome of these debates.

However, none of these limitations is an argument for restricting or setting aside liberal theses, basic rights, and principles; rather, they simply indicate that the goals and principles of liberalism, like those of any structure of political doctrines, are no guarantee of rational policy.

On the institutional level, there are no such guarantees. By the example of Tocqueville's thinking and behavior, we have seen that the orientation of the consciousness of citizens and their representatives toward the goals of freedom is indeed essential, but likewise insufficient. Political thought, whose bearings are at first set descriptively, and then is continued in the universe of prevailing opinions and convictions—"normative" in modern scientific jargon—can distinguish between right and wrong only if "common sense" is not corrupted. A politically active person is so continuously subjected to the tensions in human social life, that he must decide one way or the other, and many decisions cannot wait, so that the necessity to act quickly renders it difficult to make many decisions according to truth and justice.

The operations of a politician are not primarily characterized by a search for truth and justice. Politicians, especially in democracies, typically strive for agreement; the prevailing opinions of society always restrict a politician, or compel him to retire from the institutional-political representational process. Tocqueville's analyses and descriptions of American democracy make this clear to any open-minded reader. Any analysis of liberal democracy, which reduces this problem to the task of maintaining freedom in society, remains incomplete. A self-respecting free citizen of a republican society who jointly with his fellow citizens takes his own fate in his own hands must not be motivated solely by a love of free-dom—no matter how essential this is. His mind must be molded by objectivity toward experience and love of truth. And he must be prepared to break through the web of opinions and convictions by inquiring into the purpose and basis of political action and political order.

This business of inquiring, however, this free study, stands apart from politics. Also, the latter cannot wait. It is not only Tocqueville's oft-quoted "tyranny of the majority," but also the compulsion to act quickly which prevents politicians from testing prevailing opinions. Whoever wishes to act in politics must engage in prevailing opinions; whoever engages in opin-ions will be governed by them; and whoever permits himself to be governed by them is not guided by a love of truth and the search for justice, since his actions will be wrong to the extent that the prevailing opinions are false.

No one would in general maintain that the prevailing opin-ions in a society, or in its segments, parties, or groups (news-paper editors, for example), are always right. In concrete situ-ations this is often assumed, and this is convenient and, as a rule, successful. In the end, votes and choices are made ac-cordingly, and respect for the courage to espouse an opinion differing from the majority has done little to promote politi-cal careers.

Yet we are dealing here with more than espousals of diver-gent opinions. Whenever opinions, convictions, or "fixed at-titudes" determine the actions of citizens, that is, almost always, society runs a danger of blindly pursuing the goals that are corollaries of the "fixed attitudes." Neither the goals nor the fixed attitudes are subjects of critical inquiry.

Nonetheless, this critical inquiry is the sole safeguard for the spiritual and habitual openness of a person who is not in a position to solve the problem of his existence by reducing "truth" to axioms and thus solving the problem once and for all. The axioms so generally offered prove to be empty of meaning and faded, and of little assistance for concrete dealings.

What I wish to convey with these words is not only a problem for philosophers in ivory towers, but a general problem of human conduct. This concerns nothing less than the self-discipline of persons who, in the realm of theory, inquire into the basis and purpose of their lives and, by this inquiry, keep their minds open for practical experiences and directed to the search for truth. In the realm of conduct, the theoretically objective citizen will inquire beyond the world of opinions and convictions and subject the goals of acting to a process of serious deliberation that questioningly tests these goals as to their reasonableness in relation to human existence in society and history. It is obvious that he will not reach a conclusion, or will tend not to act at all, since the purposes of acting are not made clear. The way of life of the deliberating inquirer avoids falling into error through the actions required of the politician.

This is not a special plea for retreat from politics, but rather a statement of the problem of human conduct in society, present also in republics. For the problem of an inquiring philosophical life is that it, too, does not pierce through the domination of opinions over society by withdrawing from politics, but thereby leaves the field open to those who are not even aware of the problem of a political way of life and who therefore are much more likely to be wrong. The problem is insoluble.

Notes

TRANSLATOR'S PREFACE

1 Alexis de Tocqueville, *Democracy in America*, ed. Phillips Bradley, trans. Henry Reeve, and rev. Francis Bowen, 2 vols. (New York, 1945); hereafter cited as *Democracy* 1 or 2.

2 Alexis de Tocqueville, *The Old Regime and the French Revolution*, trans. Stuart Gilbert (Garden City, N.Y., 1955); hereafter cited as *Old Regime*.

3 Alexis de Tocqueville, *Recollections*, trans. George Lawrence and ed. J. P. Mayer and A. P. Kerr (Garden City, N.Y., 1971); hereafter cited as *Recollections*.

PREFACE

1 Reprinted in Michael Hereth and Jutta Höffken, *Alexis de Tocqueville, Zur Politik in der Demokratie* (Baden-Baden, 1981), pp. 121ff.

2 Jack Lively, *The Social and Political Thought of Alexis de Tocqueville* (Oxford, 1962).

3 George Wilson Pierson, *Tocqueville and Beaumont in America* (New York, 1938).

4 Seymour Drescher, *Dilemmas of Democracy: Tocqueville and Modernization* (Pittsburgh, 1968).

5 Marvin Zetterbaum, *Tocqueville and the Problem of Democracy* (Stanford, 1967).

6 Seymour Drescher, *Tocqueville and England* (Cambridge, Mass., 1964).

7 Richard Herr, *Tocqueville and the Old Regime* (Princeton, 1962).

8 Especially praiseworthy for this is the new work of James T.

Schleifer, *The Making of Tocqueville's Democracy* (Chapel Hill, 1980); but also the works by Irving Zeitlin, *Liberty, Equality, and Revolution in Alexis de Tocqueville* (Boston, 1971) and Pierre Manent, *Tocqueville et la nature de la démocratie* (Paris, 1982) should be mentioned here as examples of other worthwhile studies.

9 Originally published as the "Introduction" to the George Lawrence translation of *Democracy in America* (New York, 1966).

10 Max Lerner, *Tocqueville and American Civilization* (New York, 1969).

11 *Democracy* 1 and 2.

12 *Oeuvres, papiers et correspondances d'Alexis de Tocqueville* (oeuvres complètes), édition définitive sous la direction de J. P. Mayer (Paris, 1951 to date); hereafter cited as *O.C.* (M).

13 *Oeuvres complètes de Alexis de Tocqueville*, ed. Gustave Beaumont, 2d ed. (Paris, 1866); hereafter cited as *O.C.* (B).

INTRODUCTION

1 *Correspondence and Conversations of Alexis de Tocqueville with William Nassau Senior*, ed. M. C. M. Simpson (London, 1872), vol. 1, p. 123.

2 Cf. correspondence with Louis de Kergorlay in *O.C.* (M), 13:1, p. 78ff.

3 *Democracy* 2, p. 206.

4 For example, letter to Madame Swetchine of 20 Oct. 1856 in *O.C.* (B), 6, p. 350.

5 Letter to Hubert de Tocqueville of 4 Apr. 1857 in *O.C.* (B), 7, pp. 438ff., here esp. p. 442.

6 Speech on 30 May 1845 in *Moniteur Universel* (hereafter *M. U.*) of 31 May 1845, p. 1521.

7 Fragment of letter, January 1835 in *O.C.* (M), 13:1, pp. 313f.

8 Letter from Louis de Kergorlay, 23 Jun. 1832, ibid., pp. 256ff., esp. p. 257.

9 *Democracy* 2, p. 100.

10 Letter of 24 Sept. 1836 in *O.C.* (M), 13:1, p. 403.

11 Letter of 12 Aug. 1839, ibid., 13:2, pp. 63f.

12 For example, letters of 24 Sept. 1836, 4 Jul. 1837, and 9 Aug. 1837 in *O.C.* (M), 13:2, pp. 403f., 459f., 463ff.

13 Correspondence of 21 Sept. 1834–28 Sept. 1834, ibid., pp. 355ff.

14 Ibid., *Democracy* 2, p. 322.

15 Ibid., p. 333.

16 Ibid., p. 142.

17 One must remember, however, that a number of authors were victims of the delayed publication of the complete works of Tocqueville. The greater part of the documents on Algeria were not published until 1962.

18 Letter to Henry Reeve of 20 Oct. 1840 in *O.C.* (M), 6:1, p. 58.

19 Hannah Arendt, *The Human Condition* (Garden City, N.Y., 1959), p. 90; and *Vita activa* (Stuttgart, 1960), p. 95.

1. FREEDOM IN THE REPUBLIC

1 *Democracy* 1, p. 13.

2 Letter to his father of 3 Jun. 1831 in *O.C.* (B), 7, p. 24.

3 *Democracy* 1, p. 65.

4 Speech on Occasion of Reception into the Académie Française, 21 Apr. 1842 in *O.C.* (B), 9, p. 20.

5 Albert Salomon, "Tocqueville: Moralist and Sociologist" in Salomon, *In Praise of Enlightenment* (Cleveland and New York, 1963), p. 278.

6 For example, letter to Villemain of 31 Aug. 1852, Yale D IIIa; letter to Freslon, July 30, 1854, ibid.; letter to Kergorlay, 2 July 1854 in *O.C.* (M), 13:2, p. 288; letter to Beaumont of 22 Nov. 1855 in *O.C.* (M), 8:3, p. 350f.

7 *O.C.* (M), 8:3, p. 240.

8 Letter to Beaumont of 22 Mar. 1857 in *O.C.* (M), 8:3, p. 459.

9 *L'Ancien Régime et la Révolution*, 2d sec. in *O.C.* (M), 2:2, p. 344; hereafter cited as *Ancien Régime* 2.

10 *L'Ancien Régime et la Révolution*, 1st sec. in *O.C.* (M), 2:1, p. 217; hereafter cited as *Ancien Régime* 1.

11 *Ancien Régime* 1.

12 *Etat Social et politique de la France avant et depuis 1789* in *O.C.* (M), 2:1, p. 62.

13 *Ancien Régime* 1.

14 Cf. Albert Salomon, *Tocqueville: Moralist*, p. 278 and Albert Salomon, ed., *Autorität und Freiheit* (Zurich, 1935), p. 19.

15 Letter of 22 Mar. 1837 in *O.C.* (M), 6:1, p. 37.

16 R. Pierre Marcel, *Essai politique sur Alexis de Tocqueville* (Paris, 1910), p. 459.

17 Wolf Lepenies, *Melancholie und Gesellschaft* (Frankfurt, 1972), pp. 52ff.

18 See, for example, Tocqueville's observations on the mournful behavior of the parents of de Kergorlay in a letter to him of 12 Aug. 1938 in *O.C.* (M), 13:2, pp. 62f.

19 *Ancien Régime* 1, p. 170.

20 When Royer-Collard pressed the author of *Democracy in America* to continue his intellectual labors, strongly urged him not to let his talent decay in favor of practical politics, he answered his paternally well-meaning friend evasively and carried on his candidacy for parliament. In a letter of 29 June 1837 to the old parliamentarian he confessed his political ambition. "Great esteem, won by honorable means, always appeared to me the most worthy good in the world and the only one worth the sacrifice of time, strength, and the pleasures of life"; *OC.* (M), 11, p. 36. Tocqueville means the esteem of political citizens.

21 *Ancien Régime* 2, pp. 344.

22 Tocqueville, *Old Regime*, p. xiv.

23 *Etat Social*, p. 62.

24 *Democracy* 1, p. 9. See also *Ancien Régime* 1, pp. 301f., where Tocqueville points out the substitution of the "social" ties in the aristocratic order with political ties in democracy.

25 *Democracy* 1, p. 196.

26 *Ancien Régime* 1, p. 172.

27 Ibid., pp. 119f.

28 Letter to Louis de Kergorlay of 18 Oct. 1847 in *O.C.* (M), 13:2, p. 211. See also *Ancien Régime* 1, p. 302.

29 *Ancien Régime* 2, p. 344.

30 Ibid., p. 345.

31 Ibid.

32 Aristotle, *Politics*, 1253a.

33 Cf. Norbert Elias, *Die höfische Gesellschaft* (Berlin, 1969), esp. chap. 7, and E. W. Eschmann, *Die Führungsschichten Frankreichs* (Berlin, 1943), pp. 77ff. and 87ff.

34 On this and the continuing effect to the present day of this sup-

planting process, see Manfred Henningsen, *Der Fall Amerika* (Munich, 1974).

35 *Democracy* 2, p 103.

36 In *O.C.* (M), 8:1, p. 53.

37 *Ancien Régime* 2, p. 52.

38 Ibid.

39 Letter of 29 Jan. 1854 in *O.C.* (M), 8:3 pp. 195f.

40 This does not mean that those used to governing are free of passions. It only concerns the problem that, in an unstructured population, not used through daily practice to the exercise of political rights, there is a greater danger that passions will determine the political attitudes of people without such practice.

41 Aristotle, *Nicomachean Ethics*, 1103a.

42 Ibid., 1103a, 23–26.

43 See, for example, notes on the trip to Sicily in *O.C.* (M), 5:1 and earlier parts of correspondence, esp. in *O.C.* (B).

44 Ralf Dahrendorf, *Die angewandte Aufklärung* (Munich, 1963), p. 14.

45 Henningsen, *Fall*, p. 125.

46 Tocqueville stresses over and over that his true subject is not the United States of America, but democracy, and thereby the future of France. See, for example, foreword to 12th ed. *Democratie* (1848), in *O.C.* (M), 1:1, p. xliv; letter to Reeve of 15 Nov. 1839 in *O.C.* (M), 6:1, pp. 47f.; letter to Kergorlay of 18 Oct. 1947 in *O.C.* (M), 13:2, pp. 208ff.; letter to Stoffels of 21 Feb. 1835 in *O.C.* (B), 5, pp. 247ff.; letter to his father of 24 Jan. 1832 in *O.C.* (B), 7, pp. 109f.

47 *Democracy* 1, p. 61.

48 Ibid., p. 87.

49 Ibid., p. 66.

50 Ibid., p. 67.

51 Ibid., p. 66.

52 Ibid.

53 Ibid., p. 68.

54 Ibid., p. 191.

55 Ibid., p. 175.

56 Ibid., p. 182.

57 Ibid., p. 283.

58   *Democracy* 2, p. 105.

59   *Ancien Régime* 1, pp. 166f.

60   Hannah Arendt, *On Revolution* (New York, 1965), p. 115. On politics as a special form of human activity, see Bernard Crick, *In Defence of Politics* (London, 1962); August Heckscher, *The Public Happiness* (New York, 1962); and E. Vollrath, *Die Rekonstruktion der politischen Urteilskraft* (Stuttgart, 1977).

61   The following quotations, if not otherwise indicated, are taken from the chapter, "Political Effects of Decentralized Administration in the United States," in *Democracy* 1, pp. 85ff.

62   Adolf Gasser, *Gemeindefreiheit als Rettung Europas* (Basel, 1943), p. 91.

63   Hannah Arendt, *On Violence* (New York, 1969), p. 44.

64   On this problem, see ibid., and Hannah Arendt, *Vita Activa* (Stuttgart, 1960), pp. 193ff.

65   Max Weber, *Wirtschaft und Gesellschaft*, ed. Winkelmann, (Tübingen, 1956), vol. 1, p. 38.

66   Thomas Hobbes, *De Homine* (*On Man*) in *Man and Citizen*, trans. by Charles T. Wood et al. (Garden City. N.Y., 1972), p. 49.

67   Ibid.

68   Thomas Hobbes, *Leviathan*, ed. Crawford B. MacPherson (London, 1968), pp. 150ff.

69   *Democracy* 1, pp. 258ff.

70   Ibid., p. 260.

71   Ibid.

72   Ibid., p. 138.

73   Ibid., p. 276.

74   Notes on Switzerland (1836) in *O.C.* (M), 5:2, p. 176.

75   *Old Regime*, p. 256.

76   *Democracy* 1, p. 250.

77   Jack Lively, *The Social and Political Thought of Alexis de Tocqueville* (Oxford, 1962), p. 248.

78   *Old Regime*, p. 140.

79   *Democracy* 2, p. 19.

80   Ibid.

81   Ibid., p. 318.

82   Michael Oakeshott, *Rationalism in Politics* (London, 1962).

83 *Democracy* 2, p. 121.

84 Ibid., p. 123.

85 Ibid.

86 Ibid., p. 125.

87 Letter of 2 Oct. 1843 in *O.C.* (M), 9, p. 57.

88 Doris Goldstein, *Trial of Faith: Religion and Politics in Tocqueville's Thought* (New York, 1975).

89 On this, see Waldemar Gurian, *Die politischen und sozialen Ideen des französischen Katholizismus*, Mönchen-Gladbach, 1929, p. 98ff.; Hans Maier, *Revolution und Kirche*, 3d ed. (Munich, 1973), pp. 102ff.

90 Letter from Lesueur to Tocqueville of 16 Jul. 1822, Yale A IV.

91 *Democracy* 2, p. 22.

92 *Democracy* 1, p. 307; *Democracy* 2, p. 22.

93 On the description of the metaphysical revolt of 18th century thinking, see Tilo Schabert, *Natur und Revolution* (Munich, 1969).

94 For examples, see *Democracy* 1, pp. 312ff., 314; *Democracy* 2, p. 143; *Old Regime*, p. 153; *Ancien Régime* 2, p. 348.

95 *Democracy* 2, p. 22.

96 *Democracy* 1, p. 305.

97 *Ancien Régime* 1, p. 306.

98 Ibid.

99 Ibid., pp. 133ff., esp. p. 137.

100 Ibid., p. 306.

101 *Democracy* 1, p. 303.

102 Tocqueville on Seneca in a letter to Freslon of 29 Dec. 1855, Yale D IIIa.

103 *Democracy* 2, op. cit., p. 143.

104 Ibid., p. 126.

105 Ibid., p. 27.

106 Ibid., p. 34.

107 *Democracy* 1, p. 93.

108 Letter of 8 Jan. 1858 in *O.C.* (B), 7, p. 475ff.

109 See also "Introduction," *Democracy* 1, p. 13.

110 Letter to Beaumont of 2 Jan. 1858 in *O.C.* (M), 8:3, pp. 528f.

111 Letter of 29 Jun. 1831 in *O.C.* (M), 13:1, pp. 255ff., esp. p. 231.

112   For example, ibid., p. 227; *Democracy* 1, p. 43; *Democracy* 2, p. 11.

113   With these observations I interpret a number of sentences in *Democracy in America* in which Tocqueville pictures the progress of the human mind from naive religion to conviction overcoming doubt, as statements stemming from his own process of development: *Democracy* 1, p. 189.

114   *Democracy* 2, p. 20.

115   *Old Regime*, p. 153; *Democracy* 1, 143. Letter to Lord Radnor, May 1855 in *O.C.* (B), 4, pp. 44–50.

116   *Democracy* 1, p. 313.

117   Letter from Yonkers of 29 Jun. 1831 in *O.C.* (M), 13:1, pp. 225ff., esp. pp. 227f.

118   *Democracy* 2, p. 126.

119   Ibid., p. 20.

120   Ibid., p. 22.

121   In *O.C.* (M), 13:1, pp. 225ff.

122   Tocqueville asks the friend to preserve the letter; cf. last sentence of letter ibid., and footnote 1 of editor in *O.C.* (M), 5:1, p. 232.

123   The passages set forth here were also not published by Beaumont in the first edition of the works and letters of Tocqueville—which is in accord with Tocqueville's intent, it appears to me.

124   *Democracy* 1, p. 300.

125   *Ancien Régime* 1, p. 88.

126   Letter to Arthur de Gobineau of 5 Sept. 1843 in *O.C.* (M), 9, pp. 45ff., esp. p. 46f.

127   *Democracy* 1, p. 93.

128   Tocqueville, *Recollections*, New York, p. 5.

129   Ibid., p. 6.

130   *Democracy* 2, p. 133.

131   Ibid., p. 98.

132   Ibid. and passim.

133   For this, see Jürgen Gebhardt, *Die Krise des Amerikanismus* (Stuttgart, 1976), p. 238.

134   *Democracy* 2, p. 99.

135   Ibid., p. 99.

136   Ibid., p. 99.

137   Ibid., pp. 128f.

138   In the meantime, this perversion of the democratic republic and the reduction of the citizens to pursuit of comfort had also entered political thinking. A widely read work that claims to describe "democracy" realistically is witness to this, see Anthony Downs, *An Economic Theory of Democracy* (New York, 1957). On this subject, see Michael Hereth, *Freiheit, Politik und Ökonomie* (Munich, 1974), pp. 33ff.; and Lothar Kramm, *Die politische Wissenschaft der bürgerlichen Gesellschaft* (Berlin, 1975).

139   *Ancien Régime* 1, p. 175.

140   *Voyages en Angleterre, Irlande, Suisse et Algérie* in O.C. (M), 5:2, p. 91.

141   Ibid.

142   Ibid.; see also *Democracy* 1, p. 249.

143   Letter to Louis de Kergorlay of 18 Oct. 1847 in O.C. (M), 13:2, p. 211.

144   *Democracy* 2, pp. 140f.

145   Ibid.

146   *Ancien Régime* 1, p. 217.

147   *Democracy* 2, p. 229.

148   Ibid., p. 158.

149   Ibid. and, for example, *Democracy* 1, p. 425.

150   *Democracy* 2, p. 190.

151   Ibid., p. 159.

152   Ibid., p. 161.

153   Ibid., p. 160.

154   Ibid., p. 309.

155   Ibid., p. 189.

156   Letter to Louis de Kergorlay of 22 Sept. 1853 in O.C. (M), 13:2, p. 264.

157   *Democracy* 2, p. 141.

158   Ibid., p. 316.

159   Ibid., p. 317.

160   Ibid., p. 319.

161   Ibid.

162   Ibid., p. 321.

163   Ibid., p. 141.

164   In *Old Regime* he states explicitly about the Revolution: "It is still operative" (see p. 20).

165   For example, see letter to Gustave de Beaumont of 1 Feb. 1852 in *O.C.* (M), 8:3, pp. 18ff.

166   As, for example, in the otherwise extremely detailed and helpful article by Melvin Richter, "Tocqueville's Contribution to the Theory of Revolution," *Nomos*, ed. Carl J. Friedrich, 8 (New York, 1966), pp. 75ff.; or Immanuel Geiss, *Tocqueville und das Zeitalter der Revolution* (Munich, 1972), pp. 271ff.

167   *Democracy* 2, p. 13.

168   *Etat Social et Politique de la France avant et depuis 1789* in *O.C.* (M), 2:1, p. 53.

169   *Old Regime*, p. 20.

170   Ibid., p. 28.

171   Richter, "Tocqueville's Contribution," p. 82.

172   *Old Regime*, pp. 165ff.

173   *Ancien Régime* 2, p. 198.

174   Ibid., p. 45.

175   Ibid., p. 36.

176   Ibid., p. 335.

177   *Recollections*, p. 75.

178   But see his note 8 in *Ancien Régime* 2, p. 337.

179   Ibid., pp. 337f. and pp. 348f.

180   Ibid., p. 229.

181   Ibid., p. 230.

182   Cf. Geiss, *Tocqueville*, p. 275.

183   *Ancien Régime* 2, pp. 133f.

184   Ibid., p. 276.

185   Ibid.

186   See Simpson, ed., *Correspondence and Conversations*, vol. 2, p. 207.

187   *Recollections*, p. 5.

188   *Ancien Régime* 2, p. 45.

189   Speech before the Chamber of Deputies of 27 Jan. 1848 in *O.C.* (M), 1:2, pp. 348ff., esp. p. 372.

190 Letter to Beaumont of 27 Feb. 1858 in *O.C.* (M), 8:3, pp. 542ff., esp. p. 544.

191 Cf. Goldstein, *Trial*, pp. 70ff.

192 Cf. Seymour Drescher, *Tocqueville and England* (Cambridge, Mass., 1964).

2. ALEXIS DE TOCQUEVILLE: THE POLITICAL MAN

1 *Democracy* 2, p. 13.

2 Ibid.

3 *Recollections*, p. 62.

4 Ibid.

5 I will not hide behind the great Frenchman; I support his psychological explanation.

6 Albert Camus, *L'homme révolté* (Paris, 1951).

7 The confusion of language in the social sciences as a result of such a program may be an indication that the story of the Tower of Babel tells more than a story, and secondly that my surmise is correct, that the program of vain self-idolatry actually does occur with many social scientists.

8 Letter to Charles Stoffels of 22 Oct. 1831 in *O.C.* (B), 8, pp. 82f.

9 Letter of 6 Apr. 1838 in *O.C.* (M), 11, p. 59. Cf. also letter to Beaumont of 23 Mar. 1853 in ibid. 8:3, pp. 95f.

10 See letter to Mme. Swetchine of 26 Feb. 1857 in Antoine Redier, *Comme disait Monsieur de Tocqueville* (Paris, 1925), pp. 282ff.

11 Letter to Beaumont of 2 Jan. 1858 in *O.C.* (M), 8:3, pp. 528f.

12 Letter of 3 Feb. 1857 in *O.C.* (M), 13:2, pp. 324f. esp. p. 325.

13 Cf. esp. the letter to Duvergier de Hauranne of 9 Jan. 1856 in *O.C.* (B), 6, pp. 331ff. in which Tocqueville describes his procedure in detail.

14 *Democracy* 1, p. 299.

15 Letter to Corcelle of 17 Sept. 1853 in *O.C.* (B), 6, p. 227.

16 Cf. ibid., pp. 36ff.

17 For example, see *Democracy* 2, p. 334; and *Recollections*, p. 84.

18 Letter to Gobineau of 17 Nov. 1853 in *O.C.* (M), 9, pp. 201ff.

19 Letter to Beaumont of 29 Jan. 1854 in *O.C.* (M), 8:3, p. 186.

20 Letter to Beaumont of 13 Jan. 1854 in ibid., p. 182.

21　Cf. W. Hennis, *Politik und praktische Philosophie* (Neuwied, 1963), esp. pp. 89ff; and Chaim Perelmann and L. Olbrechts-Tytecta, *La Nouvelle Rhétorique* (Paris, 1958).

22　On development before and after Isocrates, as well as for him, see George A. Kennedy, *The Art of Persuasion in Greece* (Princeton, 1963).

23　On Roman rhetoric, see George A. Kennedy, *The Art of Rhetoric in the Roman World* (Princeton, 1972).

24　On this, see the very helpful study by Jerrold E. Seigel, *Rhetoric and Philosophy in Renaissance Humanism* (Princeton, 1968), esp. "Introduction."

25　Ibid., p. xi.

26　Ibid.

27　Aristotle, *Rhetoric* I, B; Seigel, *Rhetoric*, pp. 12f., 70.

28　Cf. Seigel, *Rhetoric*, p. 64 and passim.

29　Cicero, *Orator*, 70.

30　Ibid., 12.

31　The problem is likewise not solved for the philosopher. If he does not know how to influence the opinions, actions, and convictions of his fellow citizens, society deteriorates also, and his recourse is withdrawal to the school of philosophy. The search for truth, his endeavors for justice and insight become, perhaps, an historical incident without practical consequence for real society and its disorder.

32　Cicero, *Brutus*, 185, 276; Cicero, *Orator*, 69.

33　Cicero, *Brutus*, 185; *Orator*, 69f.

34　Perelmann and Olbrechts-Tytecta, op. cit., p. 27, pp. 31ff., and pp. 132ff.

35　*Democracy* 2, p. 8.

36　For proof, see Letter to Louis de Kergorlaly, 29 Jun. 1831 in *O.C.* (M), 13:1, pp. 225ff., esp. pp. 225f., where Tocqueville classes religious problems, and also "opinions" as "croyances."

37　*Democracy* 2, p. 8.

38　Ibid.

39　Ibid., p. 9.

40　In a letter to Mme. Swetchine of 26 Feb. 1857, Tocqueville speaks of his unrest that was caused by "the incessant and vain endeavors of a spirit which strives for certitude and cannot grasp it" (from Otto Vossler, *Alexis de Tocqueville* [Frankfurt/Main, 1973] p. 57).

41   In *O.C.* (B), 9, pp. 643f.

42   Ibid., pp. 123f.

43   *Democracy* 2, p. 88.

44   Report made on behalf of the *Commission chargée d'examiner la Proposition de M. de Tracy relative aux Esclaves des Colonies,* in *O.C.* (M), 3:1, pp. 40ff., esp. p. 47ff.

45   *De la Classe Moyenne et du Peuple* in *O.C.* (B), 9, pp. 514ff., esp. p. 519.

46   Letter of 21 Oct. 1839 in *O.C.* (M), 11, pp. 86ff., esp. pp. 87f.

47   Published in *Alexis de Tocqueville als Abgeordneter,* ed. Joachim Kühn (Hamburg, 1972), pp. 59f. The connection of this document to Tocqueville is unfortunately not so certain as the publisher claims. The footnote of Joachim Kühn to this document reads: "Transcript by a different hand with amendments by Tocqueville" gives the appearance of great authenticity. In fact, there is no proof that it is a transcript and not an original text (perhaps a draft). Moreover, I could not find any indication that the obvious amendments came from the pen of Tocqueville. In the immediately preceding letter Tocqueville's "vous savez depuis longtemps quelle est ma profession de foi" (ibid., p. 58) cannot be taken as indubitable proof that Tocqueville is the author of the ensuing "profession of faith." Considering the fact, however, that the content of the document actually reflects Tocqueville's position, and there are a number of exact expressions to be found, word for word, in his letter—for example, in the letter to Kergorlay of 12 Dec. 1836 in *O.C.* (M), 13:1, pp. 430f.—I tend to accept document number 40 in the Hamburg collection as a paper that was either presented to Tocqueville as a draft or was one that he dictated. In any case, the handwriting is identical with that of document 1a (ibid., p. 23 footnote) which is that of Clamorgan's pen.
I have subdivided my translation of the text by number to facilitate references to passages.

48   For example, cf. Tocqueville's letter to Royer-Collard, 29 Jun. 1837 in *O.C.* (M), 11, pp. 33ff., esp. pp. 34f.

49   *Democracy* 1, p. 7.

50   Ibid., p. 6.

51   Ibid.

52   *Old Regime,* p. 161.

53   Tocqueville formulates this especially clearly in his notes on Edmund Burke's works on the French Revolution. He emphasizes that Burke does not see the universal character and general significance

that the French Revolution has for historical development. *Ancien Régime* 2, pp. 338ff., esp. p. 341; also *Ancien Régime* 1, p. 96. Burke misunderstands the *novelty* of the Revolution.

54   *Democracy* 2, p. 334.

55   *Democracy* 1, p. 4.

56   On this, see his notes in vol. 2 of *Ancien Régime*, the paragraphs on "democracy" in *O.C.* (M), 2:2, pp. 198ff.

57   Doris Goldstein speaks about Tocqueville's didactic goals in *Trial of Faith: Religion and Politics in Tocqueville's Thought* (New York, 1975), in pp. 18, 19, 74, 76, 102, 109 and passim.

58   A few examples: *Democracy* 1, pp. 98, 104, 106, 140f.; *Democracy* 2, pp. 319, 336.

59   Fragment of letter, end Jan. 1835 in *O.C.* (M), 13:1, p. 374.

60   12 Dec. 1836, ibid., p. 431 (reproduced in original handwriting).

61   *Democracy* 1, p. 329.

62   Ibid., p. 318.

63   Ibid., p. 307.

64   Ibid., p. 329.

65   Ibid.

66   Ibid., p. 7.

67   Cf. George Wilson Pierson, *Tocqueville and Beaumont in America* (New York, 1938), pp. 737f.

68   Cf. *Democracy* 1, p. 386 and p. 417.

69   *Democracy* 2, p. 103.

70   Cf. André Jardin, "Tocqueville et l'Algérie," in *Revue des Travaux de l'Académie des Sciences Morales et Politiques*, 4th ser. (1962): 61.

71   Speech on 27 Jan. 1848 in *O.C.* (M), 1:2, p. 372.

72   Ibid.

73   Lecture at public annual conference of the *Académie des Sciences Morales et Politiques* in *O.C.* (B), 9, pp. 117ff.

74   Cf. André Jardin, André Jean Tudesq, *La France des Notables*, in *Nouvelle Histoire de la France Contemporaine* (Paris, 1973), 6, pp. 143ff.

75   Letter of 14 Dec. 1846 in *O.C.* (M), 8:1, p. 604.

76   Letter of 8 Aug. 1839 in *O.C.* (M), 9, pp. 79ff., esp. pp. 81f.

77   Letter to Ampère of 10 Oct. 1841 in *O.C.* (M), 11, pp. 151ff.

78 Letter to Beaumont of 21 Oct. 1841 in *O.C.* (M), 8:1, pp. 499ff.

79 Letter to Royer-Collard of 27 Feb. 1841 in *O.C.* (M), 11, p. 107ff.

80 J. P. Mayer, *Alexis de Tocqueville* (Munich, 1972), p. 73.

81 André Jardin, "Tocqueville député sous la Monarchie de Juillet," *Contrepoint*, No. 22-23 (1976), p. 168. The article gives a precise insight into the political career of Tocqueville.

82 Speech of 20 Jan. 1845 in *M. U.* of 21 Jan. 1845, p. 124.

83 Speech of 3 Feb. 1843, printed in *O.C.* (B), 9.

84 Speech of 18 Jan. 1842 in *M. U.* of 19 Jan. 1842, pp. 108f.

85 Speech of 3 Feb. 1843 in *M. U.* of 3 Mar. 1843, p. 350.

86 Speech of 18 Jan. 1842 in *M. U.* of 19 Jan. 1842, p. 108.

87 Speech of 27 Jan. 1848 in *O.C.* (M), 1:2, p. 370.

88 Speech of 18 Jan. 1842 in *M. U.*, 19 Jan. 1842, p. 108.

89 Speech of 27 Jan. 1848 in *O.C.* (M), 1:2, pp. 370f.

90 Speech of 17 Jan. 1844 in *M. U.*, 18 Jan. 1844, p. 92.

91 Speech of 27 Jan. 1848 in *O.C.* (M), 1:2, p. 372.

92 *Recollections*, p. 16 .

93 *De la Classe Moyenne et du Peuple* in *O.C.* (B), 9, p. 514.

94 *Recollections*, p. 12.

95 *De la Classe Moyenne* in *O.C.* (B), 9, pp. 504ff.

96 Ibid., p. 516.

97 Ibid., p. 517.

98 Ibid., p. 518. Tocqueville left open the passages in the manifesto in which he had planned his critique of Socialist systems, and formulated only the general rejection.

99 Ibid., pp. 518f.

100 *Democracy* 1, p. 242

101 Letter of 29 July 1847 in *O.C.* (B), 6, pp. 129ff.

102 Letter of 10 Sept. 1856, ibid., pp. 337ff.

103 Ibid., p. 339.

104 *De la Classe Moyenne in O.C.* (B), 9, p. 319.

105 Letter of 19 May 1849 in *O.C.* (M), 8:2 pp. 136f.

106 Speech of 12 Sept. 1848 in *O.C.* (B), 5, pp. 536ff.

107 Cf. J. L. Talmon, *Politischer Messianismus* (Köln, 1963), p. 132.

108.   Cf. the comical portrayal of his concierge in *Recollections:* "A half-crazy drunkard and good-for-nothing, who, when he was not engaged in beating his wife, spent all his time in a saloon. One can say that from birth, or better still, by character, he was a Socialist" (p. 169).

109   *Recollections,* pp. 75f.

110   In *Alexis de Tocqueville als Abgeordneter,* ed. J. Kühn (Hamburg, 1972), p. 137.

111   Letter to H. Reeve of 22 Mar. 1837 in *O.C.* (M), 6:1, p. 37.

112   Letter to E. Stoffels of 5 Oct. 1836 in *O.C.* (B), 2, pp. 435ff.

113   Ibid.

114   Letter to E. Stoffels of Mar. 1848, cited from R. Pierre Marcel, *Essai politique sur Alexis de Tocqueville* (Paris, 1910), p. 372.

115   *Recollections,* p. 168.

116   Ibid., p. 170.

117   Ibid., p. 169.

118   Letter to E. Stoffels of 5 Oct. 1836 in *O.C.* (B), 5, pp. 436f.

119   *Democracy* 1, p. 243.

120   Speech of 17 Jan. 1844 in *M. U.* of 18 Jan. 1844, p. 92.

121   Ibid.

122   Speech of 28 Jan. 1843 in *M. U.* of 29 Jan. 1843, p. 163.

123   On this, see J. Ancel, *Manuel Historique de la Question d'Orient* (Paris, 1927), esp. pp. 11 6ff.

124   Tocqueville to Thiers in 1840; citation from André Jéan Tudesq, *Les Grands Notables en France* (Paris, 1964), p. 494.

125   For example, speech of 30 Nov. 1840 in *M. U.* of 1 Dec. 1840, pp. 2549ff.

126   For example, speech of 20 Jan. 1845 in *M. U.* of 21 Jan. 1845, pp. 124ff.

127   Tocqueville develops these thoughts especially clearly in his great foreign policy on 20 Jan. 1845, ibid.

128   Ibid., p. 125.

129   Ibid.

130   Speech of 30 Nov. 1840 in *M. U.* of 1 Dec. 1840, p. 2549.

131   Ibid.

132   *Democracy* 1, p. 386.

133   Cf. Goldstein, *Trial of Faith,* pp. 70ff.

134 Ibid.

135 *Democracy* 1, pp. 331ff and pp. 356ff.

136 Cf. Seymour Drescher, *Dilemmas of Democracy, Tocqueville and Modernization* (Pittsburgh, 1968), pp. 151ff.

137 Ibid., p. 162.

138 As *rapporteur* of a parliamentary commission he presented a great investigative report: *Rapport fait au nom de la Commission chargée d'examiner la proposition de M. Tracy relative aux esclaves des Colonies* in *O.C.* (M), 3:1, pp. 44ff; hereafter cited as *Report;* and he fought in the parliament for the liberation of the slaves (ibid., p. 112).

139 In *Le Siecle* of 22 and 28 Oct., 21 Nov., 6 and 14 Dec., 1843, printed in ibid., pp. 79ff.

140 *Democracy* 1, p. 332.

141 Ibid., p. 333.

142 Ibid., p. 334.

143 Cf., for example, Eldridge Cleaver, *Soul on Ice* (New York, 1968); and Frantz Fanon, *Las Damnés de la Terre* (Paris, 1961).

144 This friend, with whom he traveled in America, who sat in parliament with him, and with whom he was a lifelong friend, wrote a famous novel as a result of his experiences in America, *Marie, ou L'Esclavage aux Etats-Unis* (Paris, 1836), the main subject of which is a bitter accusation against slavery.

145 *Report*, pp. 42 and 47ff.

146 Ibid.

147 *Democracy* 1, pp. 357f.

148 Ibid., p. 356.

149 Ibid., p. 359.

150 Alexis de Tocqueville, *Mémoire sur le Pauperisme, publié sur un rapport de M. Alfred Neymarck* (Paris, 1915).

151 Ibid., p. 7.

152 *Report*, p. 59.

153 Ibid., p. 72.

154 Ibid., p. 76.

155 Ibid., p. 57.

156 Ibid., p. 59.

157. Ibid., pp. 79ff.; see above, note 139.

158   Ibid., p. 104; see also p. 98.

159   Ibid., pp. 104f.

160   For example, *Report*, pp. 57, 59.

161   Ibid., p. 59.

162   *Democracy* 2, p. 166.

163   *Report*, p. 55.

164   See above, p. 98.

3. ALGERIA

1   Cf. Charles Julien, "La Conquête et les Débats de la Colonisation, 1827–1871," *Histoire de l'Algérie Contemporaine* (Paris, 1964), chap. 1.

2   Cf. A. J. Tudesq, *Les Grands Notables en France 1840–49* (Paris, 1964), pp. 802ff, esp. pp. 826ff., 831ff.

3   Cf. ibid., pp. 812ff., 820ff., 826.

4   Two Letters on Algeria in the newspaper, *La Presse de Seine et Oise*, 23 Jun. 1837 in *O.C.* (M), 3:1, pp. 129ff.; also 2d article, pp. 139ff; hereafter cited as Two Letters.

5   Ibid., pp. 146f.

6   Ibid., p. 147.

7   Ibid., p. 148.

8   Ibid., p. 140.

9   *Notes du Voyage en Algérie de 1841*, in *O.C.* (M), 5:2, pp. 210f.

10   Ibid., pp. 211f.

11   Ibid., p. 215.

12   *Travail sur l'Algérie* (Oct. 1841), *O.C.* (M), 5:2, pp. 213ff. and p. 221.

13   Two Letters (2d letter), p. 151.

14   *Travail sur l'Algérie*, pp. 213f.

15   Ibid., p. 215.

16   Ibid., p. 216.

17   Two Letters (2d letter), p. 153.

18   *Notes Diverses sur la Colonisation de l'Algérie*, ibid., p. 290.

19   *Rapport fait par M. De Tocqueville sur la Projet de Loi relatif aux Crédits extraordinaires demandés pour l'Algérie*, in *M. U.*, 25 May 1847, pp. 1379–1386, printed in *O.C.* (M), 3:1, pp. 308ff., esp. 309; hereafter cited as *Rapport*.

20 *Travail sur l'Algérie*, p. 227.

21 Ibid., pp. 226f.

22 Cf. Julien, *Histoire de l'Algérie*, pp. 316ff.

23 Ibid., pp. 279ff., 310f.

24 *Travail sur l'Algérie*, p. 226.

25 Ibid., pp. 226f.

26 Ibid., p. 228; see also *Notes du Voyage en Algérie de 1841*, in O.C. (M), 5:2, p. 196.

27 *Travail sur l'Algérie*, p. 228.

28 Speech on 29 June 1846 in O.C. (M), 3:1, p. 299.

29 *Travail sur l'Algérie*, p. 221.

30 Ibid., p. 236.

31 *Rapport*, in O.C. (M), 3:1, p. 328.

32 *Travail sur l'Algérie*, p. 221.

33 *Rapport*, p. 329.

34 Ibid., p. 324.

35 I find myself unable to translate the word Tocqueville uses, "justice," as *Gerechtigkeit* (justice)—Hereth.

36 *Rapport*, p. 324f.

37 The above-mentioned parliamentary commission presented together with its first report, a second one: *Rapport fait par M. De Tocqueville sur le Projet de Loi portant demande d'un Crédit de 3 Millions pour les camps agricoles de l'Algérie*, in O.C. (M), 3:1, pp. 380ff (hereafter cited as *Rapport 2*).

38 Speech on 9 June 1846 in O.C. (M), 3:1, p. 294.

39 *Travail sur l'Algérie*, p. 244; see also p. 247.

40 Ibid., p. 247.

41 Ibid., p. 248.

42 Ibid., p. 249.

43 Ibid., p. 252.

44 *Rapport*, p. 351.

45 *Rapport 2*, pp. 380f.

46 Ibid., p. 381.

47 Ibid.

48 *Rapport*, p. 329.

49 Ibid., pp. 330ff.

50   André Jardin, "Tocqueville et l'Algérie," *Revue des Travaux de l'Académie des Sciences Morales et Politiques,* 4th ser. (1962): 62.

51   Letter of Kergorlay to Tocqueville, 20 Sept. 1833; and letter of Tocqueville to Kergorlay, 11 Nov. 1833, in *O.C.* (M), 13:1, p. 339 and pp. 343f.

52   *Notes du Voyage en Algérie de 1841,* in *O.C.* (M), 5:2, for example, pp. 191, 192, 195. See also letter to Edouard de Tocqueville of 30 May 1841 in *O.C.* (B), 6, p. 112.

53   *Rapport,* for example, pp. 327f., 329f. *Rapport* 2, for example, p. 380. Cf. also Jardin, "Tocqueville et l'Algérie," p. 61.

54   For example, *Notes du Voyage,* p. 210.

55   Tudesq, *Les Grands Notables,* p. 819.

56   Ibid., pp. 802ff., 822, 833.

57   Ibid., pp. 812ff., 822.

58   Melvin Richter, "Tocqueville on Algeria," *The Review of Politics* 25 (1963): 364.

59   Ibid., p. 365.

60   Speech of 9 June 1846 in *O.C.* (M), 3:1, pp. 292ff., esp. pp. 293f.

61   *Rapport,* p. 324.

62   "Introduction," ibid., p. 32.

63   Seymour Drescher, *Dilemmas of Democracy, Tocqueville and Modernization* (Pittsburgh, 1968), p. 195.

64   Memorandum of Alexis de Tocqueville of 26 July 1835 in Kilkenny, *How Aristocracy Can Produce One of the Best or Worst Governments in the World,* in *O.C.* (M), 2, pp. 132f.

65   Speech on 9 June 1846, p. 305.

66   See the second section of the cited *Rapport,* which bears the title "Civil Administration—Government of the Europeans," pp. 330ff.

67   *Democracy* 1, p. 384.

68   Cf., for example, speech in parliament on 17 Jan. 1848 in *O.C.* (B), 9, pp. 520ff.

69   *Discours de Réception a l'Académie Française,* 21 Apr. 1842 in *O.C.* (B), 9, p. 20.

70   Letter to Ampère of 10 Oct. 1841 in *O.C.* (M), 9, p. 152.

71   Letter to Beaumont of 9 Sept. 1850 in *O.C.* (M), 8:2, p. 296.

72   *Democracy* 2, p. 17.

73   *Democracy* 1, p. 259.

Index of Persons

194   *Index of Persons*

Hobbes, Thomas, 26, 48, 178
Höffken, Jutta, 173

Isocrates, 184

Jardin, André, 117, 158, 186, 187, 192
Jefferson, Thomas, 27
Julien, Charles, 190

Kennedy, George A., 184
Kergorlay, Louis de, 5, 55, 87, 108, 174, 175, 176, 182, 184
Kramm, Lothar, 181
Kühn, Joachim, 185, 188

Lamennais, Félicité de, 126
LaMoricière, Gen. Christophe Louis, 146, 149
La Rochefoucauld, 17
Lawrence, George, 174
Lepenies, Wolf, 17, 176
Lerner, Max, 174
Lesueur, 179
Lively, Jack, 46, 173
Louis Philippe, 4, 125
Louis XIV, 26, 110
Louis XVI, 29

Machiavelli, Niccolò, 92
Madison, James, 92
Maier, Hans, 179
Manent, Pierre, 174
Marcel, R. Pierre, 17, 176, 198
Marcuse, Herbert, 75
Marx, Karl, 1, 105
Mayer, J. P., 117, 174, 187
Mill, John Stuart, 46
Montesquieu, Charles-Louis, Baron de, 89, 92
Mottley, Marie, 4

Napoleon I, 79
Napoleon (Louis) III, 4, 7, 15, 70, 79, 97, 125
Nassau, William, Sr., 174
Neymarck, Alfred, 189

Oakeshott, Michael, 46, 178
Olbrechts-Tytecta, L., 184

Perelmann, Chaim, 183, 184
Petrarch, 92
Pierson, George Wilson, 173, 186
Plato, 89, 93

Radnor, Lord, 180
Rédier, Antoine, 183
Reeve, Henry, 17, 173, 175, 188
Richter, Melvin, 158, 182, 192
Royer-Collard, Pierre-Paul, 86, 98, 115, 176, 187

Salomon, Albert, 14, 175
Salutati, Coluccio, 92
Schabert, Tilo, 179
Seigel, Jerrold E., 184
Seneca, 179
Simpson, M. C. M., 174, 182
Smith, Adam, 48, 65
Stoffels, Charles, 86
Stoffels, Eugène, 125, 183, 188
Swetchine, Madame, 123, 174, 183, 184

Talmon, J. L., 187
Thiers, Louis Adolphe, 116, 130, 188
Tocqueville, Edouard de, 192
Tocqueville, Hubert de, 174
Tracy, 185, 189
Trotsky, Leon, 105

Library of Congress Cataloging-in-Publication Data
Hereth, Michael, 1938-
Alexis de Tocqueville : threats to freedom in democracy.
Translation of: Alexis de Tocqueville.
Includes bibliographical references and index.
1. Tocqueville, Alexis de, 1805-1859. 2. Liberty.
3. Democracy. I. Title.
JC229.T8H4713 1986   321.8′092′4   85-20594
ISBN 0-8223-0541-0 (alk. paper)